Essential 1/12th & F1 RC Racer's Guide

Dave B Stevens

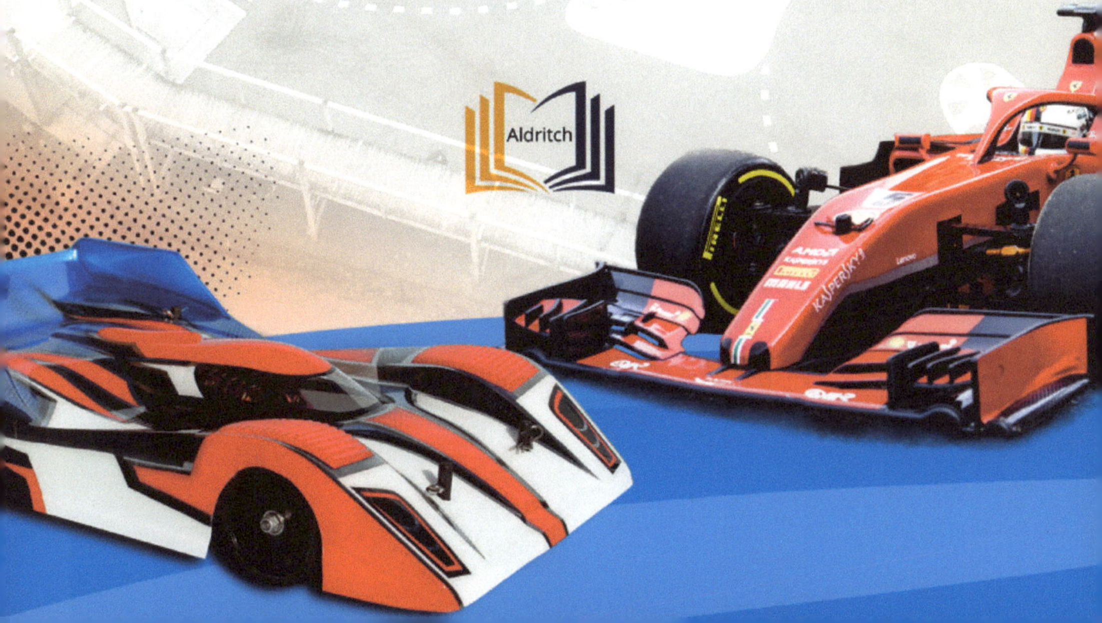

Copyright © 2019 David Bryan Stevens. www.DaveBStevens.com

All rights reserved. No part of this publication may be reproduced, stored in a retrieval system, or transmitted in any form or by any means, electronic, mechanical, photocopying, recording or otherwise, without the prior permission of the copyright holder.

Published by Dave B Stevens, Aldritch Publishing, Melbourne, Australia.

ISBN 978-0-6485811-0-9: First printed in 2019. Reprinted in 2020.
ISBN 978-0-6485811-3-0: Print on demand released 2021.

Graphic Design: Evie Diakogeorgaki
Illustrations: Ruwan Prasanga
Proof Reading: Rhiannon Raphael
Technical Contribution: David Spashett, Jan Ratheisky, Paul Sims, Andy Cooke, Aaron Stevens.
Additional Case Studies: Scott Rawlings, Ricky Vocale.
Cover Body Painting: Scott Rawlings (1/12th), Roman Fu (F1).

Photo Credits: Thank you to the following for their kind permission to reproduce their photos in this book. The page numbers for each of their photos are listed after the contributor's name (t=top; m=middle; b=bottom; l=left; r=right):

Brett Allan: 17t; George Beever: 15t, 36, 66, 99, 133t; Hugh Benbow: 75; Bradley Burge: 132, 134m&b, 135; Warren Buttriss (www.essentialrc.com.au): 59, 90, 106, 133m, 140; Henry C: 39t; Andy Cooke: 15b, 69r, 123; Martin Cranton: 79tr; Roman Fu: cover F1, title page F1, 18, 32, 61, 134t; Ernel Galsim: 105t; Will Haines: 79br; Keith Harper: 85; Historic-AG (www.historic-ag.com) 10b, 17b, 39b, 98b, 105b; Dan Maher: 20; Paul Marlan: 67; Stewart McDermott: 78l; Wayne Rabot: 78r; S37 Racing: 46, 136; Nick Sanfilippo: title page track, 121, rear cover track; Nicola Sbrana (www.nicola670paint.com) 21, 28, 35, 38, 42, 120, 131; Peter Seyfarth: 79bl; Michael Sherman (www.speedyrc.com.au): 102; Paul Sims: 112; Marcelo Souza: 79tl; David Spashett: 11, 15; Aaron Stevens: 10t, 16, 40t, 40m, 40bl, 82, 84, 86, 97, 101, 103; Bob Stormer: 37, 83; Matt Subotsch: 34, Andreas Teubl (A83 Speedgraphix): 152, 134b; Miroslav Vrana: 88; Paul Witham: 69l; Xray (www.teamxray.com): cover photo of Jan Ratheisky, 12.

All other photography is by the author.

To my wife Jackie for her support and her tolerance of my absence on race days. To my son Aaron and good mate Chris Bismire for all the amazing race meetings shared.

I would also like to thank the following for their support and advice: Grant Dixon, Chris Bismire, Hasan Ibrahim and David May (www.metrohobbies.com.au).

Table of Contents

chapter 1

Introduction — 10

1/12th Scale Foreword — 11
F1 Foreword — 12
Author's Preface — 13
Introduction — 14
How To Use This Book — 14
The Cars — 15
- 1/12 — 15
- F1 — 16

chapter 2

The Process of Driving Faster — 17

Introduction — 18
Setup Theory — 18
Setup Sheets — 20
Weight Transfer – the Holy Grail — 21
The Racing Line — 22
- Braking Point — 23
- Turn-in Point — 23
- Apex — 24
  - Wide Corners — 24
  - Geometric Apex — 25
  - Late Apex — 26
  - Early Apex — 27
  - Overtaking on a Corner — 27
  - The F1 Apex — 28
  - Hairpins — 29
  - Chicanes — 29
  - Sweepers — 30
- Slipstream Overtaking — 30
- The Position of the Next Corner — 31
- Increasing Corner Speed — 31

Mapping the Track — 33
Perfect Practice Makes Perfect — 35

Table of Contents

Driver Etiquette and Traffic 36
  Lapping 36
  Staggered Start Passing 36
  How to Pass 36
  Resolving Disputes 37
  After a Crash 37
  Hitting Someone From Behind 38
  Marshals 38

chapter 3

Car Setup Reference 39

Ackermann 41
Battery Position 43
Bodies 43
Bump Steer 44
Camber 44
Camber Gain 46
Chassis Stiffness 47
Caster 48
  Reactive Caster 49
Centre of Gravity 49
Damping 50
  Side Damping 50
    Damping Tubes 50
    Side Shock 50
  Centre Shock Damping 51
    Oil 51
    Piston Holes 52
    Rebound 52
    Springs 53
    Preload 54
    Shims 54
    Shock Length 55
Differential 55
  Ball Diff 55
  Gear Diff 57
Droop 58
  Rear Pod Droop 58

Table of Contents

   Front Droop *60*
ESC Settings 60
   1/12th ESC Settings *60*
   F1 ESC Settings *61*
Gearing & Rollout 61
   Gearing for Final Drive Ratio or Rollout? *62*
   Final Drive Ratios *62*
   Gear Ratio Charts *63*
   So What FDR Should You Start With? *63*
   What Rollout Should You Start With? *63*
   Gear Mesh *64*
   End Bell Timing *64*
   Tuning Gearing for the Lowest Lap Times *65*
   Motor Temperature *65*
Radio Settings 66
   1/12th Radio Settings *66*
   F1 Radio Settings *67*
Ride Height 68
   Overview *68*
   Measuring Ride Height *69*
   Starting Ride Height *70*
   Front Ride Height *70*
   Middle Ride Height *72*
   Rear Ride Height *72*
Roll Bars 75
Roll Centre 76
   Front Roll Centre *77*
   Rear Roll Centre *78*
Rollout 78
Shock Absorber 78
Side Links (to rear pod) 79
Springs 80
   Centre Shock Spring *81*
   Front Springs & Lube *81*
   Side Springs *82*
      Setting Side Spring Preload (Coin Trick) *82*
Steering Arm Ball-cup Location 83
Steering Linkage Angle 84
T-Bar 85
Toe 87
Track Width 89

Table of Contents

Tyres & Additives 91
   Rubber Tyres 91
   Foam Tyres 91
   Additive 92
   Tyre Warmers 93
Weight 94
   Centre of Gravity 94
   Weight Balance (Side to Side) 95
   Moving Weight (Front to Rear) 95
   Adding Weight to Increase Steering or Rear Traction 96
Wheelbase 96
Wings 97

chapter 4

Tweak **98**
What is Tweak? 99
Quick Checks 100
Rear Pod 100
Main Chassis 103

chapter 5

Case Studies **105**
Carpet Case Studies 106
   1/12th 107
   F1 114
Asphalt Case Studies 121
   1/12th 122
   F1 128

chapter 6

Other Body Shells **132**
GT12 133

Table of Contents

LMP1	134
Group C	135
Alonso & Webber Model	136

appendix A
Glossary 138

appendix B
eBook 141

appendix C
Checklists 142
   Quick Reference 142
   After Run Checks 143
   Change of Direction (Chicane) 144
   Easier to Drive – How To 144
   Fast Sweeper Cornering 145
   New Car – How to Set Up 145
   Re-building a Car 146
   Rear Traction – How to Increase 147
   Steering 148
     Too Much Steering (Oversteer) 148
        General Oversteer 148
        Oversteer at Corner Entry 148
        Oversteer at Mid-corner 148
        Oversteer at Corner Exit 149
        Oversteer On-power 149
     Not Enough Steering (Understeer) 149
        General Understeer 149
        Understeer at Corner Entry 149

Table of Contents

Understeer at Mid-corner ___ 150
Understeer at Corner Exit or at High Speed ___ 150
Steering Response Changes for No Apparent Reason ___ 150
Traction Rolling ___ 151
Troubleshooting ___ 151
Car 'Hops' or 'Chatters' Across the Track ___ 151
Car Wanders on the Straight ___ 151
Tyres Picking Up Carpet Debris from Track ___ 151
Inconsistent Handling ___ 152
Lacking Acceleration or Started Oversteering ___ 152

Chapter 1
Introduction

1/12th Scale Foreword

I started racing 1/12th in the mid-1980s, just as the UK racing scene began racing on carpet. My interest in motorsport developed into a passion for RC racing. Not just the driving and the race itself, but also the preparation and technology behind the products. 1/12th has always been my favourite class. I love the pure nature of it, striving to extract 100% from the entire package in order to be at the front.

When I first saw this book, I thought what a great idea and how useful it will be to the new drivers coming into the sport. I was impressed by the straightforward, easy to understand explanations, and the comprehensive coverage. I don't think I have ever seen an RC book with this much detail.

The future of our sport is bright, and the introduction of the IFMAR 13.5 Stock class is a great idea. However, I would like to see regulation to prevent winners from re-entering Stock at subsequent world championships, to encourage them to bring their talents to Modified.

Whether you are a Stock beginner or an experienced Modified driver, I'm sure you'll find that the information in this book can help take your racing to the next level!

David Spashett

- ✓ 3 x 1/12th IFMAR World Champion
- ✓ IFMAR Pro 10 World Champion
- ✓ IFMAR World Cup Touring Car Champion
- ✓ 14 x European Champion (1/12th, Pro 10, Touring Car and 200mm Nitro)

Author's note:

David Spashett is one of the most accomplished drivers in the world. He holds the record for the most IFMAR World Championships/World Cups won in a single season (3). David owns Zen Racing UK, an importer and distributor of racing kits and parts. He was not paid to support this book.

F1 Foreword

I've raced RC cars since the age of 6, but only at a high level for the last five years or so. When I started in F1, in the early 2000s, it was a fun second class. It is now a main professional class, and IFMAR recognised this in making it a world championship class. Many manufacturers are investing in F1, so drivers now have a great deal of choice of which kit to run.

My suggestion, as shown in this book, is to not start with a pro driver's setup. Instead, start with the manufacturer's basic setup and change it step by step. Never make more than one change at a time. Write down how the car feels in a notebook, or on your phone, and tune from there. This book provides a lot of setup information, and I hope it will help you to increase your knowledge and find good setups for yourself.

As long as you have time to practice, do it as much you can. Change, drive, repeat. Learn to feel how the car reacts before making small adjustments until the car drives the way you would like.

I drive all over the world. In the last year, this has included: Korea, Japan, USA, Australia, Philippines, China, South Africa and all over Europe. I'm pleased to report that F1 is alive and well and going from strength to strength.

Jan Ratheisky

- ✓ 2018 IFMAR World F1 Champion
- ✓ 3 x European F1 Champion
- ✓ 6 x European Touring Series F1 Champion (26 rounds won)
- ✓ 3 x International Indoor Championships F1 Champion

Author's note:

Jan Ratheisky is one of the most accomplished F1 drivers in the world. He also works full time, is the proud father of Emely and Marlon, and still manages to not only attend most of the large race events around the world but to win them! He was not paid to support this book and asked me to highlight to readers that "RC isn't my job" and that his support of this book is provided "just for fun."

Author's Preface

In 2007, my 11-year-old son, Aaron, bought an RC car on eBay. As soon as I saw it, I was hooked, and Aaron and I spent most weekends at the track from then on.

At the start of 2012, I bought a Tamiya F104 X1 and was surprised at how difficult it was to find information on how to set up and drive F1 cars. My website www.RCformula1.com went live in June 2012 to bring F1 enthusiasts information to maximise their enjoyment of this fantastic class. In the early years, it was the only dedicated RC F1 website, and it is still the most read, with nearly 6 million page views as of early 2019.

There is a lot of information on the web about setting up pan cars. However, it is often hard to find, incomplete, brand-specific, out of date or on a forum where the discussion lacks the necessary context to make it truly useful.

I wrote this book to create a comprehensive manual that racers can follow to improve their lap times, regardless of their skill level or the car they drive. I spent 30 years as a business consultant, and part of my skillset is to extract technical experience from experts in the field, pull in relevant information from multiple sources, and present it in an easy to apply "how-to" format.

About the Author

In 2013 Dave set a Guinness World Record for: The longest distance covered by a battery-operated remote-controlled car, using an F1 car (a Tamiya F104 v2).

One of the inhibitors to growing the F1 class in Australia was the lack of a national set of rules. Dave worked with racers and clubs throughout the country to rectify this and these national rules are still administered by RC Formula1 today.

Dave has been published in a number of magazines including his regular column in Racing Lines magazine. He is a former president of the Templestowe Flat Track Racers RC club and a former board member of the Victorian On Road Tracks Executive Committee. He lives in Melbourne, Australia with his wife and sons.

Connect with Dave via: Facebook   facebook.com/DaveBStevens.Author
                        Web   www.DaveBStevens.com

Introduction

The 1/12th Modified class has long been an IFMAR Worlds class. It has been joined in the last few years by the 1/12th Stock class (13.5 motor with Non-Timing ESC), and in 2018 Formula 1 became an IFMAR Worlds class (21.5 handout motor with Non-Timing handout ESC). In this book, these are all referred to as pan car classes.

Racers moving from 4WD cars to pan cars sometimes find them difficult to set up and drive. This often occurs due to a lack of understanding of pan car set up and driving techniques, and in this book, we try to provide a complete reference to these fantastic cars.

It is very achievable to have a car which has sufficient rear-end grip and still has enough steering to turn tight corners, and this guide will provide you with the information to set up the car to be both easy and fun to drive fast.

This book is also available in eBook format, for ease of access at the track (refer to page *141*).

How To Use This Book

The Process of Driving Faster starting on page *17* covers setup theory, a driving tutorial, and how to apply this theory to any track.

Car Setup Reference starting on page *39* covers the A–Z of setup settings from Ackermann to Wings and everything in between.

Tweak starting on page *98* covers how to ensure all your tyres touch the ground with equal pressure and what happens if they don't. It also describes how to fix a car that is "tweaked".

Case Studies starting on page *105* describes actual race meetings, and how skilled drivers approached their setup, what changes they made, why, and the results.

Appendix A – Glossary on page *138* defines core technical terms referred to in this book.

Appendix C – Checklists on page *142* covers all of the common problems and situations you might encounter. Car is spinning out? Wanders on the straight? Doesn't have enough steering? We've got you covered.

The Cars

1/12

- 1S Lipo battery
- Mini servo (often low profile, lightweight)
- Brushless motor: Typically 13.5 (stock) or open motor (Modified)

David Spashett's Roche P12 Evo

F1

- 2S Lipo battery
- Standard servo (often low profile)
- Brushless motor: Typically 21.5 or 25.5

Jan Ratheisky's Xray X1 2019

Chapter 2

The Process of Driving Faster

Introduction

Being able to drive faster, on a given track, is a process which involves the following steps:

1. Determine a base setup for the track.
2. Map the Racing Line for the track.
3. Practice the Racing Line for the track.
4. Tune your car's setup so that you can drive it as quickly as you are able, as close to the Racing Line as possible.
5. Practice the Racing Line for the track until qualifying starts.

Setup Theory

A car's handling is determined by the contact patch of the tyre on the racing surface. In a full-size car, the area of each tyre which touches the road is about the size of a size 10 shoe. In an RC car, this might be the size of your fingernail or smaller.

How the tyres interact with the track determines how the car corners, accelerates and brakes. So tyre choice is the most important factor in car handling. However at most large race meetings, a control tyre is used, meaning everyone has the same brand and compound of tyre. So the advantage goes to those who set up their car so that those tyres provide the right amount of grip at the right time.

Ignoring other factors for the moment, the easier the car is to drive, the faster you will be able to drive it. Changing the car's setup will make the car easier to drive near its performance limit. This should allow you to drive it faster.

In this book, we explain what each setting is, why it changes the behaviour of the car, how to make each change and the result you should expect.

Make small changes, one at a time and measure the result based on what you were trying to achieve (refer to Mapping the Track on page *33*). Note whether the car felt better or worse and any impact on lap times. We say small changes because adding a 0.5mm shim or changing a setting by 0.5 degree may make a noticeable difference, and if you jump to a 2mm shim or 1.5 degree change, then you may miss the sweet spot.

We recommend that you keep track of your setup changes and record which setups work best at different tracks under various conditions.

A car that "feels" faster is not necessarily turning faster lap times. Use a stopwatch or timing system to check if it really is quicker, and not just easier to drive.

For the car to respond correctly to setup changes, it must be in good working order. In other words: the car is not tweaked (page *98*), the suspension is free, dampers (page *50*) and differential (page *55*) is correctly built, no broken binding or loose parts, and the car has proper weight balance left to right (page *94*).

Many setup adjustments interact with other settings. For example, changing the middle ride height will also change the rear droop. These interactions are explained under the relevant headings.

Fine-tuning the setup will make the car easier to drive near its performance limit. This should allow you to drive it faster.

Start with a base setup, make changes so that the car drives the lines you want (see The Racing Line on page *22*), then stiffen the car up as much as practical while making sure it is still as easy for you to drive as possible. As you gain experience, you will be able to short cut this process.

Use our After Race Checklist on page *143* to identify problems before the next run.

Setup Sheets

Team Driver Setup Sheets can be a useful reference, and it is helpful to see what changes professional drivers have made. However, copying another driver's setup sheet without understanding why each change was made can cause a car to be undriveable: the track conditions are probably different, they may not have recorded their setup completely accurately, their driving preferences and skill level are almost certainly different to yours. Note: setup sheets are normally based on finals, once the best setup has been determined.

Different cars have unique handling characteristics. Even with the same chassis, driver style varies. That is why it is not recommended that you copy a world champion's car setup without understanding the settings. Instead, identify the differences between their setup and your car's setup and make one change at a time. Determine whether your car handling is better or worse, based on your skill level and driving style, and fine tune from there.

It is better to make small incremental changes. Most chassis will have one basic setup for carpet and another for asphalt, and this is usually a better place to start than how a pro driver sets up their car. These setup sheets may be found in your car's manual or be available on the manufacturer's website. If your manufacturer only has a carpet setup then refer to Asphalt Case Studies on page *121* for guidance on the difference between carpet and asphalt setups and how others have approached this issue.

Don't hesitate to ask for setup tips from the local fast drivers. Treat their advice like a pro driver's setup sheet by making one change they suggest at a time, and noting the result. By doing this, you are refining your own setup knowledge.

Weight Transfer – the Holy Grail

Weight transfer refers to the redistribution of weight supported by each tyre during acceleration, braking and cornering. Understanding weight transfer is the key to understanding car setup and handling.

When a car is at rest, it has a certain amount of weight on each tyre. By transferring weight from one tyre to another (front to rear or side to side), the loaded tyre will be pushed harder onto the racing surface and, therefore, will have more grip. Equally, the inside tyre on a corner will have less grip. Rapid weight transfer can alter handling characteristics, particularly if evasive action/sudden maneuver is required.

This book explains all of the setup settings available to you, how changing these will allow the transfer of more weight, or less weight, during racing and how this affects the handling of your car.

Car setup is a matter of compromise. For example, transferring more weight to the front tyres will provide more initial steering, but reduces rear traction. The objective is to set up your car so that it is easy for you to drive quickly and consistently from lap to lap while providing sufficient rear traction and sufficient steering. Of course, your definition of driving quickly will depend on your experience and skill as a driver. Regardless of how well you drive, it is possible for you to set up your car so that you can drive it as quickly and consistently as your current ability allows.

Good setup is all about controlling weight transfer.

The Racing Line

The racing line is the fastest path through any corner and identifying it is an essential skill for any driver wanting to lower their lap times.

Driving the fastest laps possible is a combination of two competing goals:
1. driving the shortest possible distance around the track, and
2. keeping the cars cornering speed as high as possible by minimising the angle of the corners.

By using all of the space available on the track, your car can travel in a straighter line and therefore drive through the corner at a faster speed (keeping in mind *Wide Corners* on page *24*).

You should experiment with different lines, watch the fast guys and talk to other drivers at the track. On some tracks, the most common racing line will show up as a darker, or even black, area on the track.

Ignoring traffic for the moment, the racing line, is determined by the following factors:

- Braking point.
- Turn-in point.
- Apex.
- The position and direction of the next corner.
- The acceleration the car has available (a Modified car's racing line may differ from a Stock or F1 car's racing line).

We will now break down each of these factors:

Braking Point

The objective when braking before a corner is to slow down just enough to be able to clip the apex. If you enter the corner too fast, you will miss the apex (understeer). If you enter the corner too slowly, you may need to accelerate mid-turn. Both scenarios mean that you won't be going as quickly as you could be.

It makes sense to brake earlier when learning the track and getting familiar with your car, then gradually reduce the braking distance as your confidence and experience grows. Ideally, you should be off the brakes before turning into the corner. For pro drivers in 1/12th, a slight brake pressure on entry can help to reduce understeer and provide a better turn-in (this is known as trail braking). With F1 it is very difficult to trail brake, and it is recommended to only brake in a straight line.

Other factors include:

- Modified motors have greater braking power than Stock class motors.

- 1/12th cars are more stable under braking than F1 cars (refer to *F1 Radio Settings* on page *67* for brake settings advice).

- Braking too early may result in a slow lap.

- Braking too late may result in overshooting the corner and a slow lap (or in the worst case scenario, a broken car).

Turn-in Point

To get the racing line right, it is vital to turn-in at the correct point. Leave it too late and you'll understeer, missing the apex. Turn-in too soon and you'll clip the apex/curb, upset the car and have to adjust your line mid-corner, losing speed.

Pick a spot on the track as your turn-in point and note it on your track map (refer to *Mapping the Track* on page *33*). Adjust this turn-in point with practice until you're happy with your line through the corner.

Apex

The apex is the point at which you are closest to the inside of the corner (also known as the clipping point). Once you have hit the apex, you should be able to reduce your steering input and begin to increase the throttle as the car exits the corner.

In general terms, there are three different types of apex. These are summarised in the table below, and you would normally select the best apex for a given corner depending on traffic and the position of the next corner:

Geometric Apex	Late Apex	Early Apex
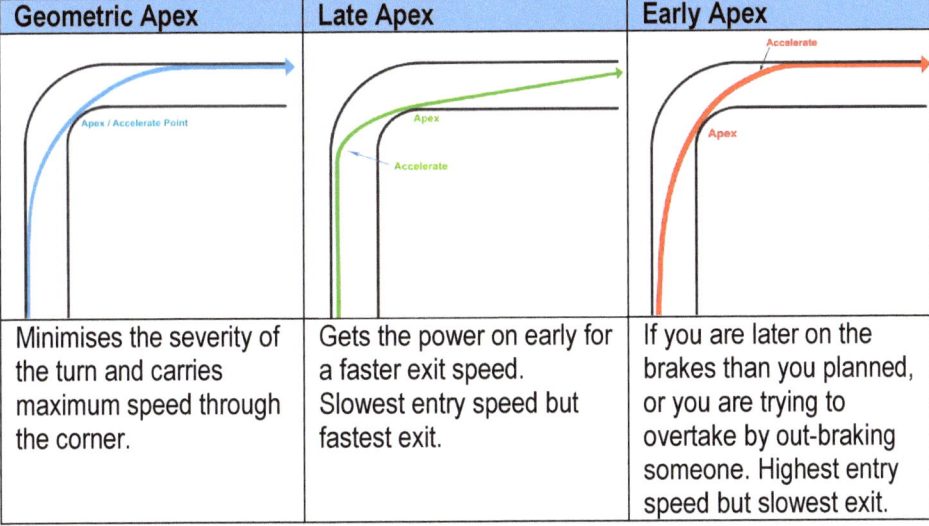		
Minimises the severity of the turn and carries maximum speed through the corner.	Gets the power on early for a faster exit speed. Slowest entry speed but fastest exit.	If you are later on the brakes than you planned, or you are trying to overtake by out-braking someone. Highest entry speed but slowest exit.

As previously stated, by using all of the space available on the track, your car can travel in a straighter line and therefore drive through the corner at a faster speed.

Each of the above is discussed in more detail on the following pages.

Wide Corners

In real racing, using the full width of the race track is normally faster, but in RC this is not necessarily the case. Refer to the optimal line around the example track on page 34.

If the entry or exit of a corner is very wide (the track width is wider than required for the racing line) then touching the outside of the track on the way in and the outside of the track on the way out simply increases the distance travelled and slows the overall lap time. In this situation, some trial and error may be required to determine the optimum position for turn-in.

Any part of the track that is not on the racing line is often dirty, with reduced grip, and should be avoided.

Geometric Apex

The geometric apex of a constant radius corner is the central point on the inside of the corner.

Hitting the geometric apex is good for carrying speed and minimising turn severity.

The fastest way through a 90 degree corner is to touch the outside of the track on the approach, hit the geometric apex of the corner and then swing out in an even curve to meet the outside edge of the track. By following a symmetrical, curved line you will be able to take the corner as fast as possible by minimising the tightness of the corner. This minimises cornering force, thereby freeing up grip for maintaining speed.

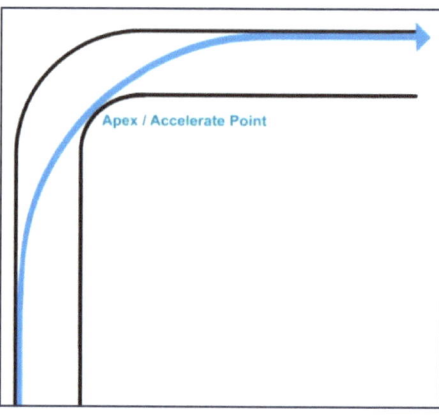

The geometric apex is exactly halfway around this corner.

Advantages:

- Smooths out the corner efficiently.
- Maintains momentum (particularly useful for Stock/lower powered cars).
- Reduces the chances of understeer or oversteer (especially helpful in low grip conditions).
- Preserves tyre life.

Disadvantages:

While it is the fastest way to drive the current corner, it is not necessarily the fastest way to drive the next part of the track and therefore won't necessarily produce the fastest possible lap times in all situations.

Late Apex

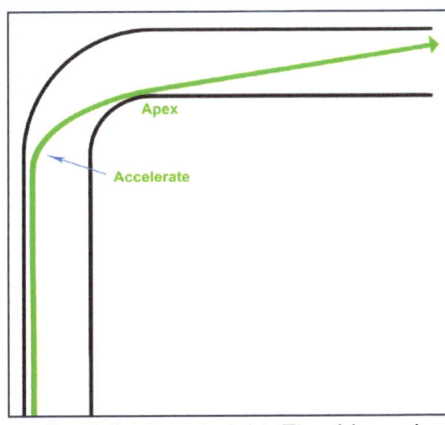

If a straight follows the corner then the ideal racing line for maximum speed over the corner, plus the straight, is a late apex. Although the car is slower into the corner when compared to a geometric apex, it positions the car to accelerate much earlier. Overall the time over that part of the track, from the corner entry to the end of the straight, is quicker.

Accelerating early as the car passes the clipping point means that it will be faster down the following straight. The driver who accelerates sooner and/or harder has a large advantage, and a late apex may assist in maximising that advantage.

Advantages:

- Increases the chances of a fast lap in a powerful car (Modified).
- Allows the power to be applied earlier.
- Maximises the use of any straights following the corner.
- Allows late braking.

Disadvantages:

- May not be the fastest path in a lower powered car.
- Places greater demand on the tyres.

Early Apex

An Early Apex can be faster for an understeering F1 car.

It can also be used for overtaking as described below.

Overtaking on a Corner

We've seen that the fastest way around a track is to follow the racing line. If you are closely following a car that is following this racing line, then they may approach the corner from the outside of the track. This provides an opportunity to brake late and take an early apex (the red racing line below), darting up the inside of your opponent. Although you will probably run wide to maintain your corner speed, you should have nosed in front of the other car. You may also have disrupted their concentration and/or forced them off the line that they wanted to take. Pass accomplished.

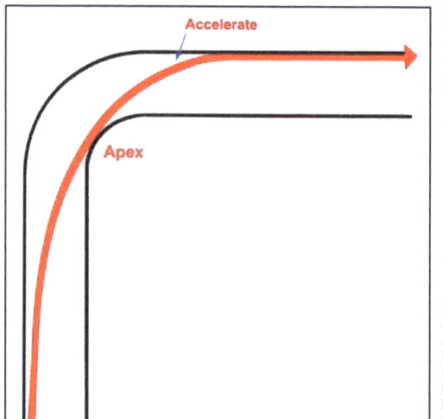 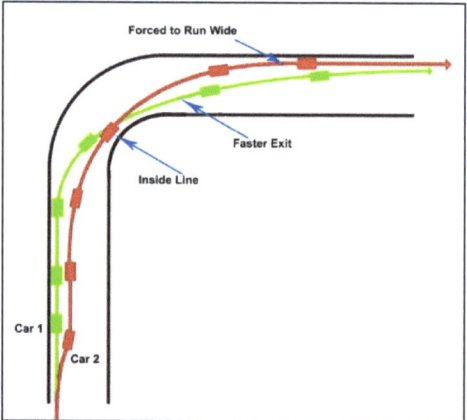

To defend against the above, you need to take a late apex while slowing sufficiently not to hit the car passing you, and then accelerate early and shoot back past them while they are running wide.

Of course, once you have another car close on your tail, you leave yourself open to the above passing scenario if you stick to the racing line. You may, therefore, wish to drive closer to the inside of the track to prevent the above overtaking move. Your choice to not drive the racing line will slow your lap times, but by not leaving a gap, you should retain the position.

The F1 Apex

Compared to 1/12th cars, an F1 is a low-powered car. Even if you install a more powerful motor than the standard 21.5 brushless motor, an F1 doesn't usually generate sufficient grip to be able to transfer that power to the track.

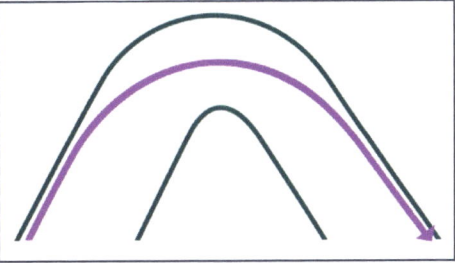

Therefore the best racing line for an F1 car can be the Karting Line. This is a wider line that doesn't hit the apex. Karts don't have particularly good brakes or very quick acceleration and therefore focus on maintaining momentum around the track. This works well for F1.

The Karting Line can also be used by faster cars when traction is low as it maintains as much momentum as possible without relying heavily on acceleration.

Driving Tips:

- Only brake in a straight line and don't jam the brakes on. Pump the brakes a couple of times to prevent the wheels locking and the car spinning.
- Don't accelerate too hard out of corners or you'll lose the back end.

F1 rewards a very smooth style on the trigger. Avoid hard transitions from full brake to full power back to full brake. Squeeze on the power.

If you can't turn as tightly as you would like, slow down. Otherwise, overshooting a corner will more than lose any gain from entering the corner faster. Then adjust your setup for the next run so that you have sufficient steering to take the corner the way you want to.

Hairpins

A hairpin is a corner which changes the direction of the car by 180 degrees. The fastest line around a hairpin is a very late apex (about three-quarters of the way around the bend). A guide point is that halfway through the turn, you should be roughly in the middle of the track.

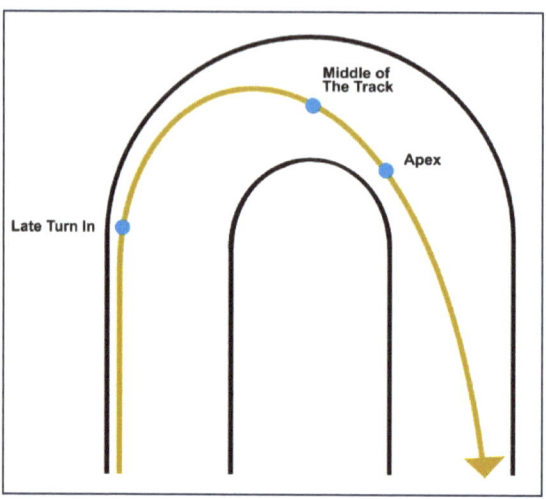

Chicanes

A chicane is a shallow corner in one direction followed by a shallow corner in the other direction. Depending on the corners preceding and following the chicane, it can often be driven at high speed. This requires a car which will change direction quickly (refer to page *144*) and examination of the chicane for the straightest possible line through it (refer to the examples on page *34*).

Sweepers

A sweeper is a long corner. Because the corner is not very sharp, the steering input is less, and because of this, the corner may be taken much faster than a sharper corner.

With some sweepers, it is faster to follow the corner as closely as possible, while with others, running wide may lead to a faster exit. Unfortunately, it is not practical to provide diagrams for every scenario.

Sweepers are often at the start or end of the straight.

If the sweeper is entered relatively slowly, because of the prior corner, then you are often accelerating during the majority of the sweeper and may be able to hug the inside throughout and still be at full speed as early as possible on the straight — example on the left below.

If the sweeper is entered at high speed, then it may be easier to think of the sweeper as two separate corners — example on the right below.

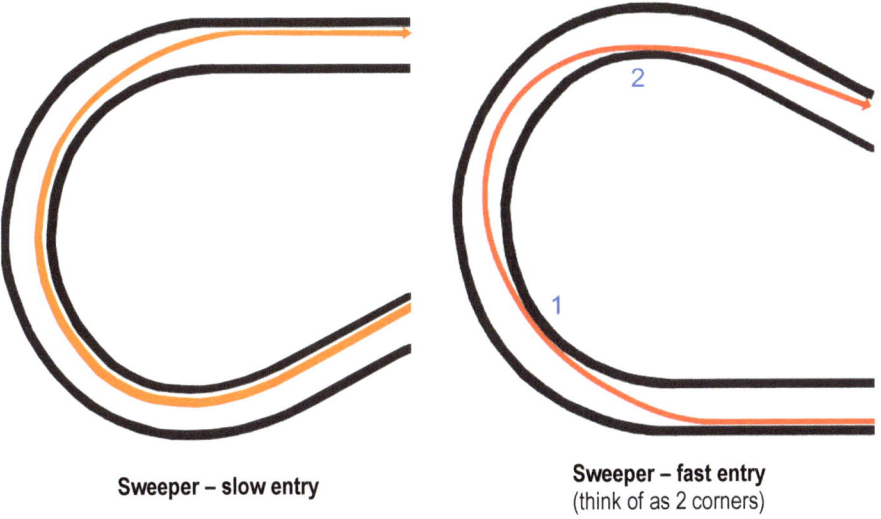

Sweeper – slow entry

Sweeper – fast entry
(think of as 2 corners)

Diagrams are examples only and will not apply to every sweeper.

Slipstream Overtaking

In RC racing, using the slipstream of the car in front is not commonly practised at club level. It is very difficult to get right, and the straights are not usually long enough for it to make a significant difference. There are exceptions but in general, tucking your car closely in behind the car in front is difficult and risky to both cars in RC.

The Position of the Next Corner

The fastest way through a 90 degree corner is discussed above under the heading Geometric Apex. However, we aren't just trying to take one corner as fast as possible, we're trying to drive a complete lap as fast as possible, and the position and direction of the next corner affect the racing line of the current corner. For example, if the next corner is a left-hander you'll need to move over to the right-hand side of the track (orange line below), and therefore will need to apex later and take a tighter, slower line. However, if the next corner is another right-hander a wider faster line can be used (red line below):

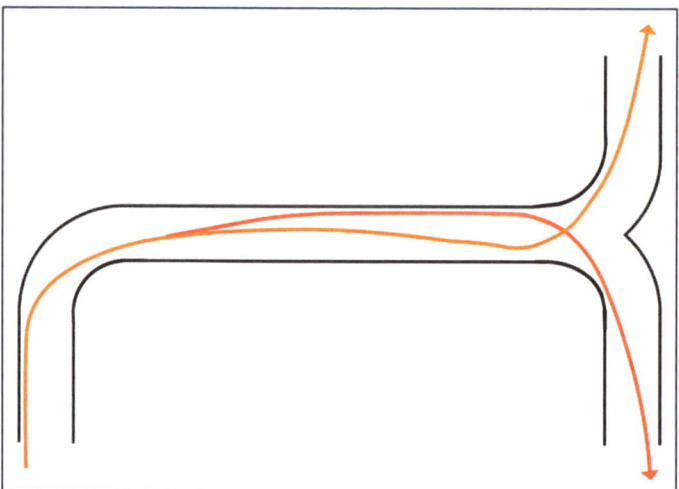

When there is a series of corners, it is better to view them as one large corner and focus on maximising your exit speed from the last corner. The early apex technique maintains car stability so that you can navigate these multiple corners. The last corner is then taken with a late apex for maximum acceleration.

Increasing Corner Speed

Now that we know how to find the best line through a corner, the next step is to drive it as quickly as possible.

"Slow in, fast out" is the strategy of slowing more on the approach to the corner to ensure that you hit your apex and get back on the throttle as soon as possible. It is a useful mantra to keep in mind when first learning about cornering. However, we don't actually want to enter the corner slowly. We only want to slow the car the minimum amount so that we can hit the chosen apex.

The fastest lap means always driving your car on the absolute limit of the available grip. When you brake, you should leave the braking as late as possible so that you can use all of the available grip to brake the car down to the speed you wish to take the corner (which is ideally the fastest speed that your car is able to take the corner). When you stop braking, this makes grip available for turning (which is why hard braking and turning at the same time can make you lose control, as well as scrubbing off speed). As you pass the apex, reduce the steering input to make grip available for acceleration.

Sections of a Corner

Ideally, braking should be smooth and fluid. Steering should also be smooth and fluid. Sudden or jerky braking/steering can upset the balance of the car, causing it to oversteer or understeer.

Tapping the brakes transfers weight forward for cornering which gives the car more grip available for steering.

The perfect corner involves tightening the steering until the apex and then gradually reducing the steering as you accelerate. If you find yourself increasing or correcting the steering during the corner, after the initial turn-in, you've probably taken the wrong line.

The greatest demand on the tyres' grip occurs between the turn-in point and the apex. It is important not to accelerate or brake during this part of the turn; you want to maintain a constant speed.

When accelerating, you will not be able to use all the power of a Modified car until you're completely in a straight line. However, if you're in a less powerful car, you can apply the throttle much closer to the apex.

Smooth braking and steering are factors that separate the professional driver from the club racer.

Mapping the Track

Now that you know how to determine the racing line for any given corner (refer to page 22) you should sketch out the racing line for the entire track. This is your map of the track. Then practice driving it. Once you are comfortable that you are driving the racing line as close as possible, it may become obvious that the car is not following the racing line in certain sections as closely as you wish. By changing the setup of the car, you can make it easier to drive the racing line. For example, the car may not follow the sweeper the way you'd like, or it may take hairpins too wide. These issues may be corrected by changing the car setup to allow you to drive the racing line you have selected more closely and therefore reduce your lap times.

Refer to *Appendix C – Checklists* on page 142 for how to correct various issues with car handling.

Walking the track can be a useful way of determining the racing line. This technique is particularly useful in chicanes to determine the straightest path through. When walking the track don't walk on the racing line itself as you may track dirt or dust from your shoes over it, changing the grip level.

On most tracks, your car will spend more time in the low-speed corners than in high-speed corners or on the straight. Therefore, that is where your biggest time gains might be made. For that reason, you may wish to adjust your gearing (refer to page 61) to increase acceleration out of corners, at the expense of top speed on the straight.

The Process of Driving Faster

Putting it all together:

The following racing line (in green) is a good starting point for F1, 1/12th Stock and Modified, and can then be adjusted to suit your skill level and driving style.

The example track is quite wide in places, and it would be much slower to use the full track width when cornering (as discussed under *Wide Corners* on page *24*).

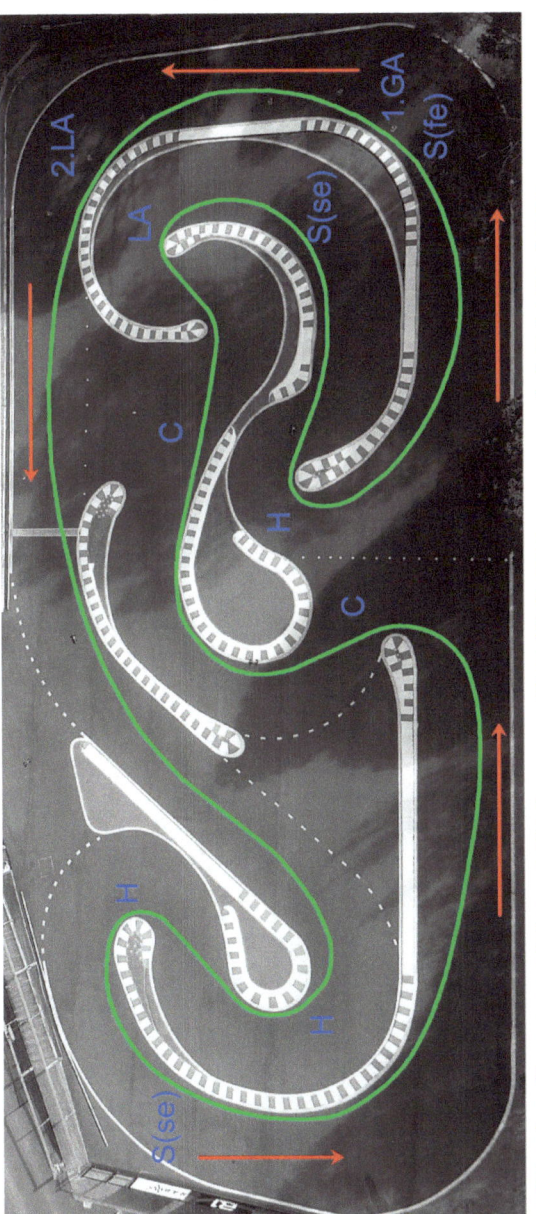

LA = Late Apex
S(fe) = Sweeper (fast entry)
(broken down into 2 corners)
GA = Geometric Apex

C = Chicane
H = Hairpin

S(se) = Sweeper (slow entry)
H = Hairpin

Refer to the Racing Line section for corner descriptions.

Perfect Practice Makes Perfect

Practice can be broken into two types:

- Driving Practice – learning the track and practising: braking, cornering, and acceleration.
- Testing – where you identify areas of the track where your car's handling could be improved, changing the setup and re-testing to see if the change is better or worse.

Experienced drivers will often combine these two types of practice, but when learning, it can be easier to focus on one or the other.

Practice is only useful if done as close to race conditions as possible. If you use tyre additive and tyre warmers at a race meeting, then make sure you do this when practising. If you are practising for an event, then use the same brand and model of tyres for practice that you will use during the event. Otherwise, you may be wasting your time as your car's grip is likely to be completely different.

Fast cornering takes practice. Identify the racing line you want to take and practice it. Change the setup of your car to make your ideal racing line as easy and fast to drive as possible. It is often easier to focus your practice on getting one or two corners right each lap rather than trying to get every corner perfect. Once you are happy with the corners you've been practising, focus on the next couple of corners. The goal, of course, is to lower your lap times.

Practising the way you will race and focusing on getting one corner right at a time until you can string them all together is "Perfect Practice", hence the title of this section.

Driver Etiquette and Traffic

Any time your car is involved in an incident, you are losing time. This section covers proper driving etiquette and how you can use it to prevent incidents.

The following provides guidance on how to handle common situations when racing:

Lapping

Drivers that are being lapped must give way to the lapping car. The race software may call cars that are about to be lapped when they cross the start/finish line, but of course, the leaders can catch people at other parts of the track. It can sometimes be confusing as to whether you are being lapped or not. If you are lapping someone and they are not moving aside then call out "red car lapping blue car", for example, so that the blue car knows the situation. The blue car must allow the red car to pass without blocking them. Of course if you are racing for position and not being lapped then block away.

Staggered Start Passing

Staggered starts for qualifying (also called IFMAR Called starts) which are used at most large events and also at some club meetings, creates an interesting situation when passing or lapping. This is how it works.

If you wait until your name or car number is called before starting, then it is a staggered start. During staggered start qualifying you are racing the clock rather than the other cars on the track. Your personal timer starts when you cross the start/finish line for the first time and ends when the race software calls the end of the race plus the lap you are on (always keep going until your name, or car number, is called as finished). The fact that other cars are on the track is irrelevant to you; it is only done to save time. Of course, if someone blocks you in this situation, then that can hurt your qualifying. You must not block people in staggered start qualifying. If someone catches you, then let them pass. Note that with staggered starts you should let people pass if they are quicker than you, whether they are lapping you or not.

How to Pass

How to let other cars pass deserves some discussion. When you are learning to drive, it can be difficult to move out of someone's way without crashing. The best way to let someone pass is to go slightly wide at a corner. Sudden changes in speed or direction can cause a crash. Slowing down suddenly might cause the passing car to crash into the back of you. If you let the person know when you will go slightly wide, then they can take advantage of it to pass. If the lapping car is Blue, then say "pass me on the inside Blue car at the next corner" or simply "inside Blue car". If you know the person's name, then use it to be even clearer e.g: "inside Jim". The passing racer will appreciate it, and it will have the least impact on your own qualifying time.

Resolving Disputes

You may have heard the term "hacked" or "taken out", for example, "he hacked me". This slang means that the person feels that someone crashed into them. If there is a racing incident that affects you, why not speak to the person involved immediately after the race? Racers who are new to the hobby sometimes need guidance on what is acceptable behaviour. As long as this guidance is provided in a positive and friendly manner, then most of the time, the person will change their behaviour. Sometimes people get angry in the heat of the moment. Walking away and trying to talk to them later, when they've cooled down, often works. If the behaviour continues, then notify the Race Director.

After a Crash

If you cause an accident, then the correct behaviour is to wait for that person to continue before you continue. An apology after the race never hurts either. We should all be aware that the speeds and distances involved mean that mistakes happen and that's racing. It's how we handle it that matters.

Hitting Someone From Behind

If you hit someone from behind, then it's always your fault. You control where your car is at any given time on the track. If the car in front brakes unexpectedly then that may well cause an incident, but the fact that you ran into the back of them is your fault. If you are coming up behind someone you've never raced with before, then it pays to be more cautious.

Marshals

If your car has left the track or is on its roof then hopefully a marshal will assist you as soon as possible.

If a marshal doesn't see your car is in trouble, then a single call of "Marshal" is acceptable to draw their attention to it. Remember that if you hadn't crashed a marshal wouldn't be necessary, so treat marshals with the respect they deserve.

The marshal's priority is to not cause issues for the drivers who haven't crashed. So marshals will not rush in front of other cars on the track to get to your car. Nor should you expect them to try to fix any issues with your car.

When your car is back on the track, do not pull out in front of another car. Wait until there is a gap.

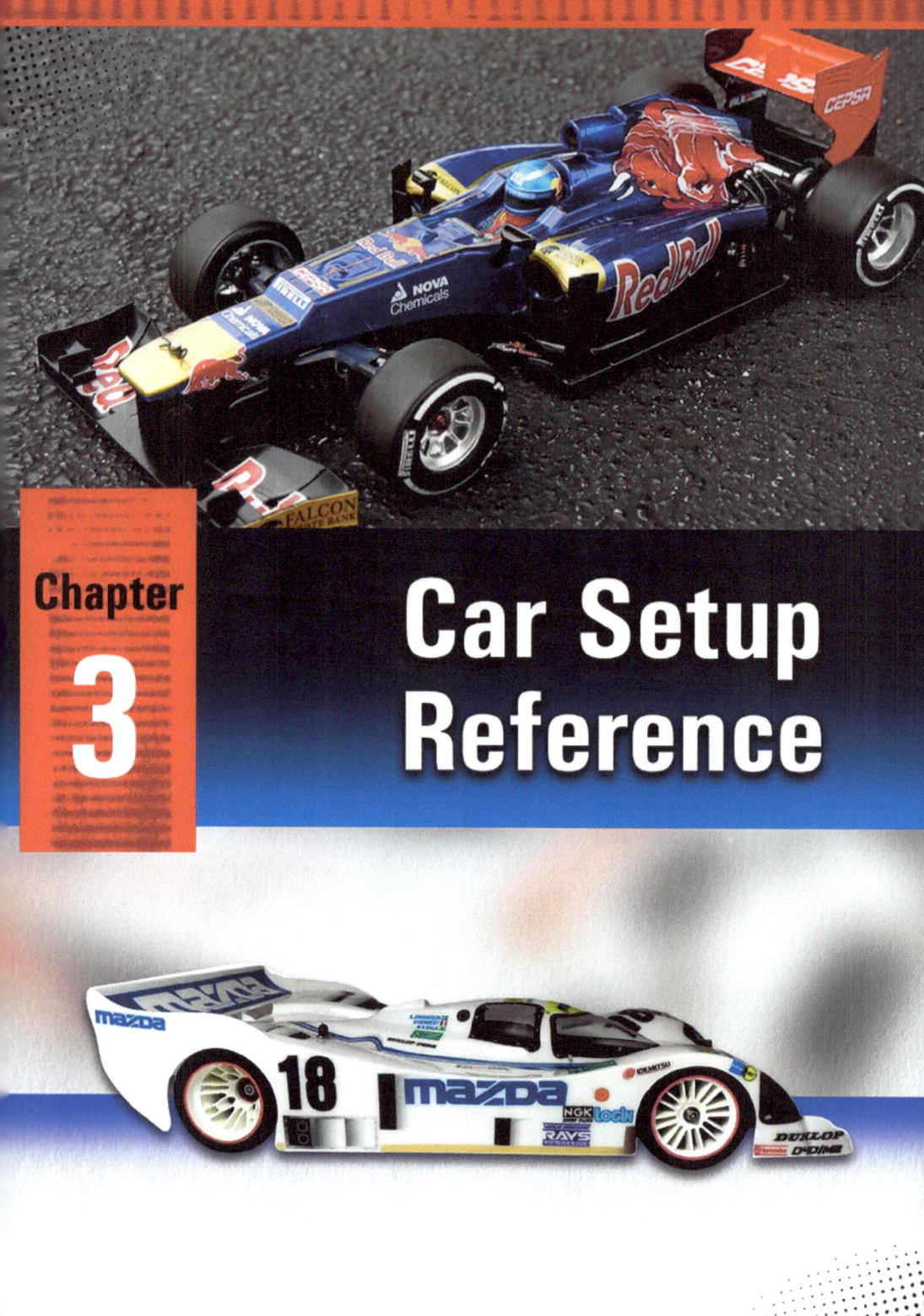

Chapter 3

Car Setup Reference

Car Setup Reference 3

This chapter covers the A–Z of setup settings from Ackermann to Wings and everything in between. Where a term used in this chapter is not explained, refer to the *Glossary* on page *138*.

This chapter refers to parts of the car as follows:

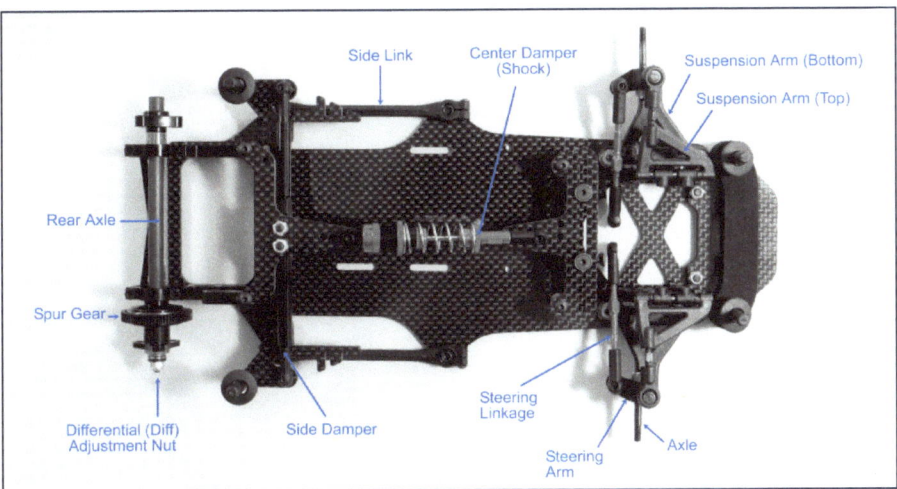

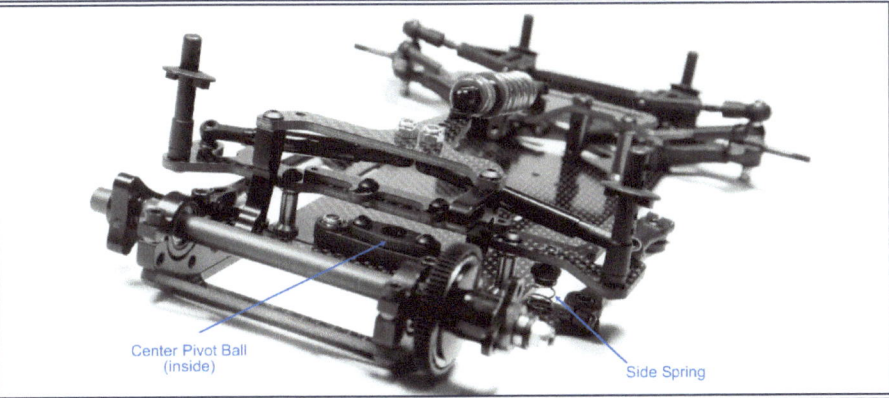

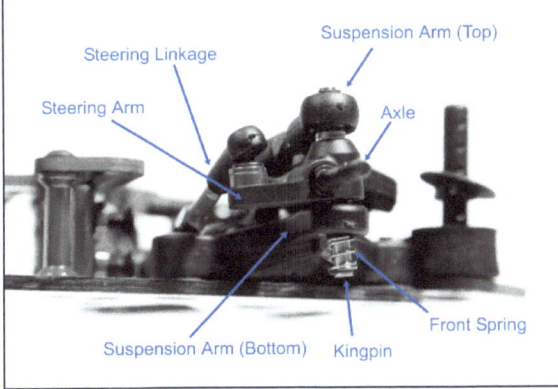
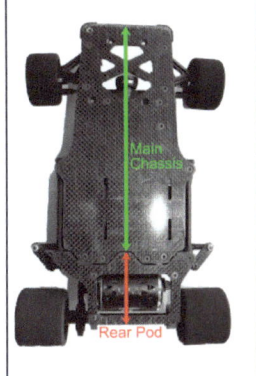

40

Ackermann

Put simply, the front inside wheel always has a tighter arc in any corner than the front outside wheel (refer to illustration). Think of it in terms of the outside of the car having further to go than the inside of the car when turning.

The Ackermann setting achieves this by controlling the geometric arrangement of the steering linkages; effectively the inside tyre turns more than the outside tyre (refer to the illustration).

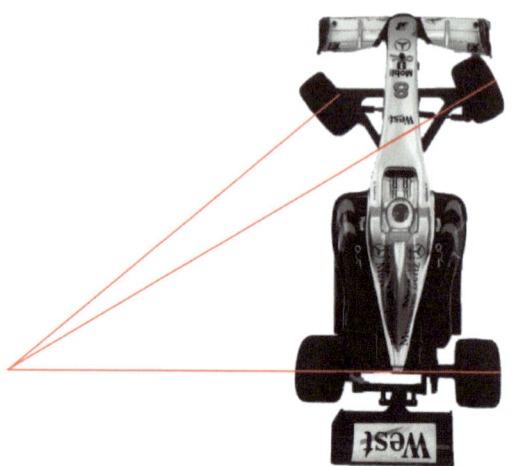

The Ackermann position is changed by moving the steering arms closer to, or further from, the front of the car. Some cars allow this to be done in two locations as shown in the photo below (green and red). The front of the car is at the top of the photo:

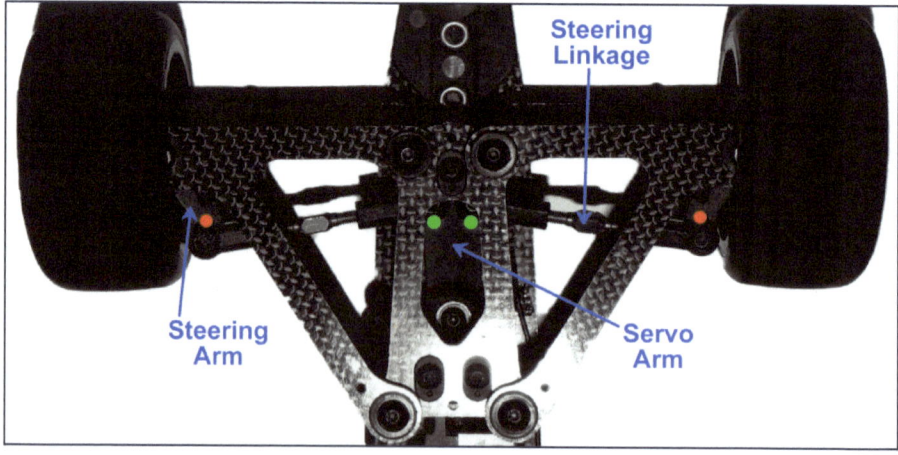

The steering linkages are connected to the servo arm in the centre of the car. The linkages are shown in the forward position (this manufacturer's kit position) but can be changed to the green holes (less Ackermann).

The car shown has a second way of changing Ackermann, on the steering arms. The linkages are currently in the rear position (this manufacturer's kit position) but can be changed to the red holes (more Ackermann).

A car's kit setup will usually suggest an Ackermann position where the car is easy to drive. Using a hole closer to the front of the car will increase Ackermann and therefore increase steering; however, the car may be harder to drive.

Some cars use shims rather than different hole locations to change Ackermann.

Setting	By Changing	Handling Impact
More Ackermann	Use a hole closer to the front of the car or increase shims to bring steering linkages closer to the front of the car.	• More initial steering into the corner. • Less corner speed. • Less traction in the chicane.
Less Ackermann	Use a hole further away from the front of the car or decrease shims to bring steering linkages further away from the front of the car.	• Less initial steering into the corner. • More corner speed. • More traction in the chicane.

Another setting for changing the steering feel is the Steering Linkage Angle on page *84*.

Interaction

Front Toe angle (refer page *87*) impacts the effectiveness of Ackermann changes.

Battery Position

If your chassis allows the battery to be moved forward or rearward on the chassis then:

Setting	Handling Impact
Forward battery position (Recommended in F1 for wide outdoor asphalt tracks)	• Car is less stable. • More initial steering. • Less mid-corner steering. • More rear traction.
Rearward battery position (Recommended in F1 for carpet tracks with a lot of braking)	• Car is more stable. • Less initial steering. • More mid-corner steering. • Less rear traction off-power.

You may also have the option of the battery being across the chassis or inline.

Setting	Handling Impact
Inline battery	Higher corner speed reduces chance to "diff out" (refer to Differential on page 55). Better for high traction conditions.
Cross-chassis battery	More neutral handling, makes car less sensitive to setup changes, reduced steering response. Better for low and medium traction conditions.

There may also be the opportunity to move the battery more to the left or right to assist with left/right weight balance.

Bodies

1/12th

Different bodies provide different handling characteristics. For examples refer to *Case Studies* on page *105*.

It is not recommended to mount the body higher or lower at the rear to change handling. Always mount the body parallel to the ground.

F1

Refer to Wings on page 97.

Bump Steer

Refer to Steering Linkage Angle on page 83.

Camber

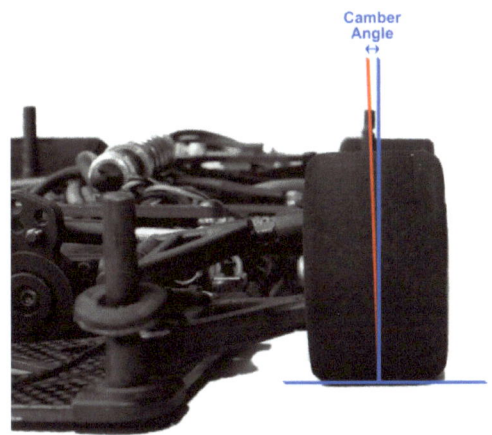

Camber angle is the angle at which the wheel leans in towards the chassis (negative camber) or away from the chassis (positive camber). In 1/12th and F1 we always deal with negative camber, as shown in the illustration, and can only change the front camber.

As a general rule, increasing negative camber improves grip on the outside wheel when cornering, thereby increasing steering (within limits, too much negative camber can reduce grip).

Visualise the car as it corners, transferring weight to the tyres on the outside of the corner, i.e: when taking a left-hand corner weight is transferred to the right-hand tyres, and when taking a right-hand corner weight is transferred to the left-hand tyres.

As the weight is transferred to the outside tyres, the car leans towards those tyres. With the correct camber angle, the bottom of the outside front tyre will be flat, or close to it, as the car corners. This maximises the contact patch of the tyre with the racetrack, resulting in the most grip and therefore the most steering.

A rubber tyre tends to roll on itself when cornering. If the tyre had no camber, the inside edge of the tyre would begin to lift from the track, reducing the contact patch.

With any negative camber this effect is reduced, thereby maximising the contact patch.

With a 4WD car, there is a compromise between steering and maximising straight-line acceleration, as the greatest traction will be attained when the camber angle is zero, and the tread is flat on the road. Because 1/12th and F1 cars are rear wheel drive, there is no compromise required.

The greater the negative camber angle, the more steering the car has. However, it makes the car more sensitive and harder to drive.

Interaction

After you set the Camber, re-check the Ride Height and the Toe setting. Conversely, after changing the Ride Height re-check the Camber.

1/12th

Front camber is normally adjusted by shortening or lengthening the front upper turnbuckles:

Change	How	Effect
Increase Camber (wheel more angled)	By shortening the turnbuckle	More steering, car more sensitive to steering inputs
Decrease Camber (wheel more upright)	By lengthening the turnbuckle	Less steering, car less sensitive to steering inputs

It is important that camber is the same for the front left and front right tyres.

Check camber frequently. If the front tyre is "coning" (the foam tyre is wearing more at one end, usually the outside, making the tyre look like a cone), increase or decrease the camber until the tyres wear flat.

1° of negative camber is a good starting point. Increasing to 1.5° may provide a noticeable increase in steering.

F1

Camber is usually fixed using blocks. It is unlikely to change, due to wear, when using rubber tyres. 1° of negative camber is a good starting point. Increasing to 1.5° may provide a noticeable increase in steering.

Camber Gain

Camber gain is how much the camber angle changes as the suspension is compressed. Camber Gain is also referred to as "camber rise" or "camber intake".

Camber gain can only be changed on the front of a 1/12th car and is not usually able to be changed on an F1 car at all.

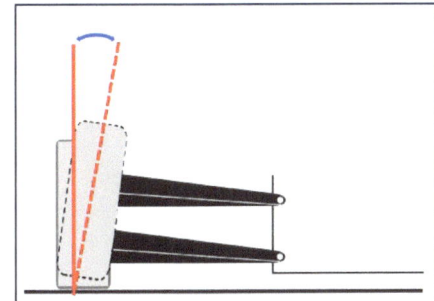

Camber gain is determined by the length of the top and bottom suspension arms (or turnbuckles) and the angle between them. If the top and bottom suspension arms are parallel and the same length, camber will not change as the suspension is compressed. If the angle between the arms is large, or the length of top and bottom arms is different, the camber will increase as the suspension is compressed.

A certain amount of camber gain is desirable to maintain the face of the tyre parallel to the ground as the car rolls into a corner.

Change	Shims	Effect
Reduced Camber Gain	More shims	Reduced initial steering and reduced sensitivity to steering inputs
Greater Camber Gain	Less Shims	Increased initial steering and increased sensitivity to steering inputs

Refer to your car's manual for shim locations. Use the same thickness shims on both sides of the car.

Interaction

Higher caster angles will increase camber gain in cornering. Refer to *Caster* on page *47*.

Camber gain interacts with roll centre to a point, although it may not be noticeable. Refer to Front Roll Centre on page *75*).

Chassis Stiffness

Chassis stiffness is an important factor when setting up your car. Some cars have the option of using a thicker carbon fibre chassis to reduce flex. Others offer an aluminium chassis to virtually eliminate flex.

Typically chassis that provide flex are better for low grip tracks, as they generate more traction and increase in-corner steering, while chassis with less flex are better for high grip surfaces. An aluminium chassis may provide better steering and stability at high grip tracks.

A stiff chassis also assists in eliminating chassis flexing and twisting, which may introduce another factor that is not easy to measure or adjust.

Your car may have setup options which fine-tune the chassis stiffness by changing the mounting of components such as the servo. Refer to your owner's manual.

Car Setup Reference

Caster

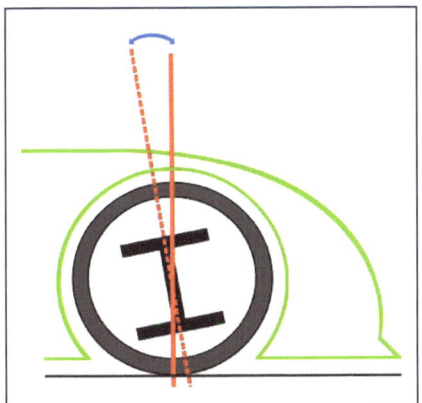
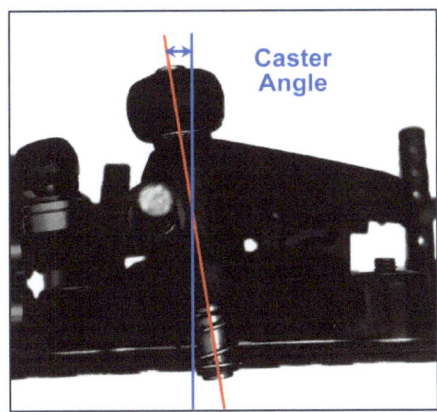

Caster Angle

Caster is the angle that the front kingpin leans to the rear of the car from the vertical (vertical being a line perpendicular to the ground). The Caster angle affects on and off-power steering, as it impacts the amount the chassis tilts.

Technically, the pivot points of the steering are angled so that a line drawn through them intersects the track surface slightly ahead of the contact point of the tyre. The purpose of this is to provide a degree of self-centring for the steering (the wheel casters around so that it trails behind the axis of steering). This makes a car easier to drive and improves its straight-line stability (reducing its tendency to wander). Excessive caster angle will make the steering heavier and less responsive.

Change	Effect
A lesser Caster angle (kingpin more upright)	Is better on slippery, inconsistent or rough tracks. Decreases traction rolling. May decrease steering.
A greater Caster angle (greater kingpin angle from the vertical)	Is better on smooth, high traction tracks. More steering overall but the car may be harder to drive. Increases chance of traction rolling.

Higher caster angles will increase camber gain in cornering.

Refer to your chassis manufacturer's manual for instructions on changing Caster angle. Both 1/12th and F1 cars normally have the ability to change this setting. On some cars, option parts may be required.

Reactive Caster

When the front of the car is rising (under acceleration), or diving (under deceleration), the Caster angle will change. Reactive Caster allows you to adjust the amount of change. Your car probably has some Reactive Caster built-in (refer to your car's manual).

Change	Effect
Increasing the Reactive Caster angle	• Will make the car react faster. • Increased corner entry steering. • Reduced mid-corner steering.
Decreasing the Reactive Caster angle	• Will make the car easier to drive smoothly when entering corners. • Car has more consistent steering through the corner.

F1 cars do not normally have the option to change this setting.

Centre of Gravity

Refer to page 94.

Damping

Damping controls the travel speed and resistance of the suspension. An undamped car will oscillate up and down on its springs. With proper damping levels, the car will settle back to a normal state in the minimum amount of time.

Side Damping

Damping Tubes

Most cars use side damping tubes (either one or two tubes). Where two tubes are used they should be the same length and use the same type and quantity of oil. Oil range is typically 10k cSt (low viscosity/thin oil) to 50k cSt (high viscosity/thick oil):

Lower viscosity oil (thinner)	Higher viscosity oil (thicker)
• Side to side transition (chassis roll) is quicker. • Increases steering. • Reduces rear traction. • For higher grip tracks.	• Side to side transition (chassis roll) is slower. • Reduces steering. • Increases rear traction. • For lower grip tracks.

Many tubes have slots for adding oil; where this is the case it is normal to add oil only in the slots, not on the whole tube. Refer to your car's manual.

Once you have the viscosity oil that you are comfortable with, you can fine tune the feel of the side damping tubes by changing the angle of the tubes with shims:

Change	Effect
Lesser Angle (tubes are closer to horizontal)	Softer feel, provides more chassis roll
Greater Angle (tubes are further from the horizontal)	Harder feel, provides less chassis roll

Side Shock

Some cars use an oil-filled shock absorber for side damping, and some offer it as an option. Typically the side shock provides more grip in low to medium traction conditions, while the side damping tubes are better for high traction conditions. The side shock does not have a spring. Changing the shock oil has the following effect:

Lower viscosity oil (thinner)	Higher viscosity oil (thicker)
• Side to side transition (chassis roll) is quicker. • Increases steering. • Reduces rear traction. • For higher grip tracks.	• Side to side transition (chassis roll) is slower. • Reduces steering. • Increases rear traction. • For lower grip tracks.

Interactions

Choice of side springs also affects side damping (refer to page *82*).

Centre Shock Damping

The Centre Shock, also called the Rear Shock, moderates weight transfer front to rear. It also damps the car over bumps. A well damped car rides the bumps smoothly.

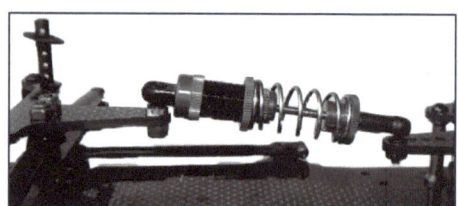

Oil

The kit oil usually works well in most conditions, but thicker or thinner oil can be used for fine-tuning:

Lower viscosity oil (thinner)	Higher viscosity oil (thicker)
• Faster shock action. • Faster weight transfer. • Suspension works faster and smoothly keeps tyre in contact with track (more traction). • Absorbs the bumps better and therefore better at bumpy tracks. • Car is more likely to become unsettled with sharp direction changes such as a chicane. • Shifts balance to the rear, providing more rear traction. • Takes longer to accelerate out of the corner as the suspension compresses further. • Car may wander.	• Slower shock action. • Slower weight transfer. • More stable at high speed and more twitchy at slow speed. • Does not deal with bumps well and therefore better at smooth tracks. • Car is less likely to become unsettled with sharp direction changes such as a chicane. • Shifts balance to the front, providing more front traction and therefore steering. • Takes less time to accelerate out of the corner as the suspension compresses less.

Piston Holes

The kit number of holes in the shock piston usually works well in most conditions, but changing the number of holes in the piston (or keeping the same number of holes but changing the hole size) can be used for fine-tuning:

Change	Effect
Fewer holes or smaller holes	• Less oil can pass through the piston as it moves. • Provides harder damping – reacts like using thicker oil. • Greater resistance to shock movement and therefore greater damping with slower shock movement.
More holes or larger holes	• More oil can pass through the piston as it moves. • Provides softer damping – reacts like using thinner oil. • Less resistance to shock movement and therefore less damping with faster shock movement.

Rebound

Remove the damper spring and push the shock shaft all the way into the shock body. When you let it go, the amount the shock shaft rebounds out of the shock body is the amount of rebound. If it doesn't move at all then rebound is 0%, if it comes out half way it's 50% and if it rebounds fully then it's 100%. Rebound may be any percentage from 0–100%.

Rebound can be used to fine tune the feel of the car. Some pro drivers prefer less rebound or even 0% rebound.

Change	Feel of the Car
More Rebound (higher %)	- Makes the car feel more responsive. - Car will be "bouncier" over bumps.
Less Rebound (lower %)	- Makes the car feel less responsive. - Car will be less "bouncy" over bumps and therefore easier to drive on a bumpy track.

To Set Rebound

1. Assemble the shock as per the manufacturer's instructions. This will normally provide 100% rebound.
2. Release the shock cap by 2–3 turns.
3. Push the shock shaft fully into the shock body. Depending on the design of the shock, oil will probably release through the overflow hole in the shock cap.
4. Tighten the shock cap. Oil will normally release through the overflow hole in the cap.
5. Test Rebound.
6. Repeat steps 2–5 until you obtain the rebound % you prefer.

Springs

The kit spring usually works well in most conditions, but a harder or softer spring can be used for fine-tuning:

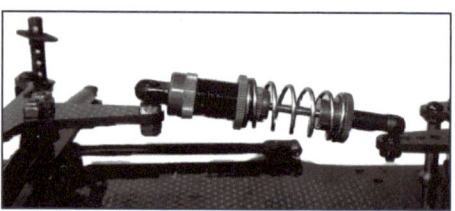

Change	Effect
Softer spring	- More weight can be transferred to the rear. - Greater rear traction. - Better handling over bumps - Reduces acceleration out of the corner. - Greater off-power steering. - Less on-power steering.
Harder spring	- Less weight can be transferred to the rear. - Less rear traction. - Worse handling over bumps. - Better acceleration. - Less off-power steering. - Greater on-power steering.

Damping oil and springs work together. If you use thinner oil, consider a softer spring. Similarly, thicker oil works better with a harder spring.

Preload

Spring preload is set by screwing the collar above the spring so that the spring is more compressed or less compressed. This changes:

1. The Middle Ride Height (refer to page 72) [the recommended use for preload].
2. It also affects the Rear Pod Droop (refer to page 58).

Compressing the spring using the preload collar does not change the force applied by the spring. However, if you compress the spring further than the natural weight of the car does, you are reducing the travel of the shock (and therefore the travel of the rear suspension).

Shims

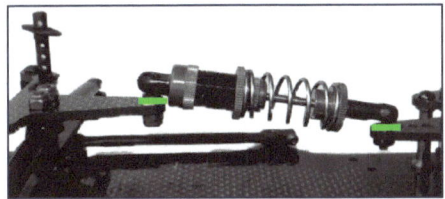

Changing the angle of the shock can make a significant difference to the traction available at each end of the car:

Change	Effect
Flatter/Less Shock Angle (less shims at the rear or more shims at the front)	• Shock does more work and has a greater impact as angle reduces. • Less weight is transferred to the rear. • Less rear traction. • Greater on-power steering.
More Angled/Greater Shock Angle (more shims at the rear or less shims at the front)	• Shock does less work and has a reduced impact as angle increases. • More weight is transferred to the rear. • Greater rear traction. • Less on-power steering.

Shock Length

Some kits allow the shock length to be changed:

Change	Effect
Longer Shock	- Improves driveability over bumps, improves on-power traction. - Less steering response, slower direction changes.
Shorter Shock	- Decreases driveability over bumps, reduces on-power traction. - Greater steering response, faster direction changes.

Differential

The wheel on the outside of a turn always has to travel farther than the inside wheel. The front wheels turn at different angles to allow for this (refer to Ackermann on page 41). The rear wheels use a differential, or diff, to allow the wheels to turn at different speeds and this assists the car to rotate into corners.

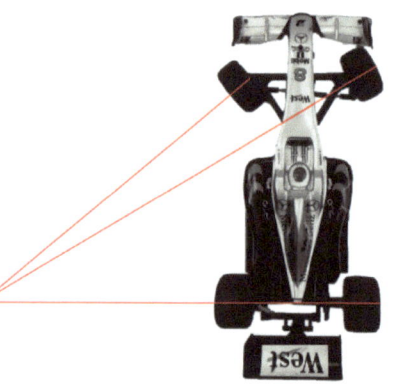

Ball Diff

Setting	Handling Impact
Tighter diff	Better acceleration, harder for the car to rotate into the corner.
Looser diff	Less acceleration, easier for the car to rotate into the corner.

How Tight Should the Diff Be?

I tighten the diff with a wrench so that it is tight (without cranking down), then let off 1/4 of a turn. For a tighter diff let off less than a quarter turn, for a looser diff let off more than a quarter turn. A tight diff may turn the motor over when you check the diff action.

Check the Diff Action

Put the car on the stand and turn the right wheel clockwise. The left wheel should turn anti-clockwise. If it doesn't, then check you have assembled your diff as per the manufacturer's instructions. The diff should feel reasonably smooth. It is not necessary for the diff to be perfectly smooth with no gritty feel at all, but the smoother the diff feels, the better it will perform.

Running in the Diff

After re-building the diff, and before checking the diff tightness, run the diff in by holding one of the rear wheels and providing a little bit of throttle to spin the other wheel. Don't run at full throttle and don't run for more than a couple of seconds. Then hold the other wheel and do the same thing.

Checking the Diff Tightness

Method 1: Hold the spur and right wheel with your right hand and use your left hand to try and turn the left wheel. The left wheel should be very difficult to rotate.

Method 2: While holding the rear wheels with your hands, use your right thumb and index finger to rotate the spur gear. The spur gear should be very difficult to rotate.

If the result is not as above, then tighten or loosen the diff nut slightly and re-test until the desired result is achieved.

The "Diffing Out" Problem

Put your car on a stand so that all the wheels are off the ground. Hold one of the rear wheels and apply some throttle.

You should notice that the wheel you aren't holding will spin twice as fast as it normally would for that amount of throttle.

Imagine that the wheel you are holding is the wheel on the outside of the corner and your car is leaning on this wheel. This outside wheel has most of the weight of the car, giving it more traction, and the inside wheel will have less weight on it and therefore less traction, allowing it to possibly break traction and start spinning. This is a "diff out" and will cause your back end to oversteer.

Thicker diff fluid or a tighter ball diff will assist to prevent "diffing out".

Ball Diff Rebuild

The ball diff should be rebuilt periodically, typically when it feels "gritty" when rotating one rear tyre by hand, or if it is no longer smooth, indicating it may need re-greasing.

Rebuild by disassembling and thoroughly cleaning the various parts of the diff. Check the diff rings. If they have a line scored into them by the diff balls then replace, or remove the line by sanding the diff rings using 600 grit wet and dry sandpaper. Wet the sandpaper with brake cleaner and sand the rings in circles until the groove is removed. Clean rings with brake cleaner and a rag after sanding.

Gear Diff

Some manufacturers offer gear differentials as an option. They are also available from third party suppliers.

Gear diffs require significantly less maintenance than ball diffs but use oil viscosity for adjustments rather than a simple nut. The manufacturer should provide a recommended starting point for oil viscosity. Modified cars tend to require thicker oil:

Setting	Handling Impact
Higher viscosity oil (thicker)	<ul><li>Used for higher traction conditions.</li><li>Used for modified cars.</li><li>Better acceleration.</li><li>Harder for the car to rotate into the corner.</li></ul>
Lower viscosity oil (thinner)	<ul><li>Used for lower traction conditions.</li><li>Less acceleration.</li><li>Easier for the car to rotate into the corner.</li></ul>

Droop

Also sometimes referred to as "downstop".

Rear Pod Droop

The main chassis and rear pod move independently around a pivot-ball with side links. Hence the term Pivot-Ball Link rear suspension.

Changing the Rear Pod Droop

There are two methods of changing the rear pod droop:

1. Change the shock preload, or
2. Change the shock length [recommended].

We recommend the second option: Changing the Shock Length. This is because the first option (changing shock preload) changes the Middle Ride Height. We recommend setting the rear pod droop by changing the shock length and then fixing the Middle Ride Height using the shock preload (refer to page 72).

Increasing the shock length by 0.5mm should increase the droop by approximately 0.5mm.

(Note: Droop is measured when the car is race ready – including tyres and battery)

Setting	Shock length	Handling Impact
Increase Droop	Increase	• Car turns in harder. • More high-speed steering. • Improves handling over bumpy tracks. • >1mm on bumpy asphalt tracks.
Decrease Droop	Decrease	• Car drives smoother into corners. • Worse handling on bumpy tracks. • <1mm or even 0mm on smooth carpet tracks.

Interaction

Changing the droop will change the Ride Height. Refer to Ride Height Interactions on page 75.

Measuring Droop

1. **Option 1 – Using a Droop Gauge** – Place the main chassis on blocks so that it is parallel to the table and so that none of the tyres touch the ground. The back of the rear pod should "droop" towards the table.

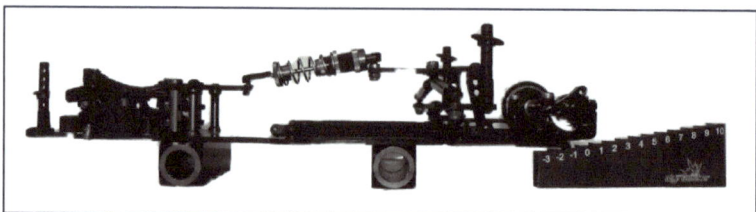

(Note: Droop is measured when the car is race ready – including tyres and battery)

By using a droop gauge, it is possible to measure this droop. 1mm is a typical starting point (as shown above) but check the manual for your car. Therefore the rear of the pod drops 1mm when the suspension is unloaded (i.e: the car is on blocks). When you place the car back on its tyres the main chassis and rear pod should form a straight line. The rear suspension therefore has 1mm of travel to transfer weight when the car accelerates or brakes.

2. **Option 2 – Using a Ride Height Gauge** – If you don't have a droop gauge you can measure the ride height at the edge of the rear pod closest to the front of the car, i.e: underneath where the side link connects. Then push down on the rear of the pod. This causes the front of the rear pod to angle upwards (or alternatively lift the car using two fingers either side of the rear of the centre shock, until the rear wheels almost leave the ground). Now measure the ride height again at the same place. The difference in the two ride height readings is the rear droop.

Front Droop

Some kits have shims to increase or decrease the front droop (refer to your car's manual).

Note: Changing the droop will change the Ride Height. Refer to Ride Height Interactions on page 75.

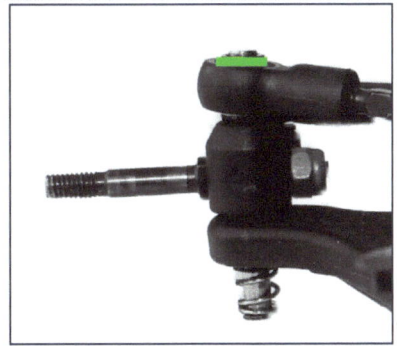

Setting	No. of Shims	Handling Impact
Increase Droop	Less shims	• Car is less reactive. • More front grip and therefore steering. • Less consistent to drive. • Better on bumpy tracks.
Decrease Droop	More shims	• Car will change direction more quickly. • Less front grip. • More on-power steering. • Better on smooth tracks.

ESC Settings

Reverse is illegal for racing, so disable it. Some ESC's will come with instant reverse, meaning that if you put the brakes on the car will instantly go into reverse. This is a real problem as it causes the car to spin.

"Blinky" denotes a mode of the ESC with no dynamic timing. This is often indicated by a blinking light on the ESC – hence "Blinky". It is also referred to as "non-timing mode".

1/12th ESC Settings

The Stock class requires the ESC to be in Blinky mode (see above for definition). There are no restrictions for the Modified class.

F1 ESC Settings

Most rules worldwide require the ESC to be in Blinky mode (see above for definition).

Drag Brake – Turn off drag brake. You only want brakes applied when you are ready for them; otherwise, the car may veer to one side or possibly spin. Some F1 racers use drag brake to assist the car to rotate into a corner, but I prefer to tap the brake if needed.

Brake Strength – Set brake strength to 100% and then reduce the brake EPA on the radio until you are comfortable with the brake force (refer to page 67).

Throttle – Set the aggressiveness of the throttle on the ESC to a medium or midway setting. In a 4WD car, running the same motor on an aggressive setting assists with acceleration. With an F1 car, you need to feed the power on as only the rear wheels are driving the car and grabbing a handful of trigger will probably cause the car to spin.

Gearing & Rollout

The correct gearing is essential to minimise your lap times. Gearing determines both acceleration and top speed.

The "best" gearing for you depends on your driving style, the track environment and the motor/chassis setup. It is therefore likely that you will change your gearing for different tracks. A large flowing track might benefit from higher top speed, while a smaller and tighter track might benefit from better acceleration out of the corners.

Gearing for Final Drive Ratio or Rollout?

Both 1/12th and F1 cars have a Final Drive Ratio (FDR) often called "gear ratio" or "ratio" or "gearing". FDR is the number of times the motor must turn so that the wheels turn once. Expressed as a ratio e.g: 4.0:1 means the motor turns four times to rotate the wheels once.

However, if you use foam tyres (as is normal in 1/12th) then you most likely use Rollout rather than FDR. Rollout is how far the car will move forward with one revolution of the motor. This depends on your FDR and the diameter of the tyres. As tyre diameter reduces, the work the motor does changes. TQ RC Racing has an excellent Rollout Calculator (www.tqrcracing.com).

Tyres	Wear	FDR or Rollout
Rubber	Minimal	FDR
Foam	Significant reduction of tyre diameter (by mm per race meeting)	Rollout

Final Drive Ratios

FDR's in pan cars tend to be lower than in a 4WD car. Pan cars are lighter and only two-wheel drive, which puts less strain on the motor and allows a lower FDR.

Lower FDR's provide higher RPM and therefore faster top speed, but less torque and therefore slower acceleration. Lower means "less than" so 3.0:1 is lower than 4.0:1.

Higher FDR's provide lower RPM and therefore slower top speed, but more torque and therefore greater acceleration. Higher means "greater than" so 4.0:1 is higher than 3.0:1.

Calculating the Final Drive Ratio (FDR)
FDR = Internal Ratio x (Spur / Pinion)

Nearly all pan cars are direct drive, that is, the pinion meshes to the spur which drives the rear wheels. There are no other gears in the drive train, and therefore the Internal Ratio is 1.0 and so can be ignored. The calculation can therefore be simplified to:

FDR = Spur / Pinion

For example, an 80 tooth spur gear with a 35 tooth pinion provides an FDR of 80/36=2.22. This means 2.22:1 or the motor turns 2.22 times for every 1 time that the wheels turn.

Gear Ratio Charts

It can be handy to make your own gear ratio charts to refer to. There are a large number of websites that will create a chart based on a range of spur and pinions you specify. For example: Gear Machine (www.gearmachine.net).

So What FDR Should You Start With?

Class	Motor	Starting FDR
F1	Silver Can Brushed	3.7:1
F1	25.5 Brushless	2.4:1
F1	21.5 Brushless	2.9:1
F1	17.5 Brushless	3.2:1

NB: for 1/12th refer to Rollout below.

21.5 (Non-Timing ESC) is the most common motor wind worldwide, although some areas or race meetings do vary.

Many racers will use a lower FDR than shown above. However, the above is a good starting point.

Things you should consider when setting your FDR:

- Motor (see table above).
- Track (open with long straight = lower, or short and tight = higher).
- Whether you have advanced the end bell motor timing (see below).
- Air temperature (see Motor Temperature below).

What Rollout Should You Start With?

Rollout is how far the car will move forward with one revolution of the motor.

Rollout is more often used with foam tyres as it takes into account tyre wear to provide accurate gearing. Simply change the pinion gear as necessary to maintain the same Rollout.

Calculating the Rollout
(Tyre Diameter x 3.14) / (spur gear / pinion gear)

Class	Motor	Starting Rollout (Slow corners and/or short straight)	Starting Rollout (Fast corners and/or long straight)
F1 (foam tyres)	21.5 Brushless	65mm	75mm
1/12th Stock	13.5 Brushless	80mm	90mm
1/12th Modified	4.5 Brushless *	35mm	40mm

* Any motor can be used in Modified. Starting rollout has been provided for a 4.5 turn motor; the smaller the number of turns, the lower the rollout.

Gear Mesh

Setting the correct gap between the pinion gear and the spur gear is vital. If the gap is too large the spur gear will strip, if the gap is too small the spur will cause drag on the pinion (often accompanied by excessive gear noise and motor overheating). Some sources suggest 0.3mm of play between the spur and pinion gear teeth. However, this is difficult to measure. If you shine a torch on the mesh, you should see a very small gap. Another option is to run a small piece of paper between the gears by turning the spur gear. It should feed all the way through and drop out. If it won't, then the mesh is too tight. Lastly, you can hold the pinion and rock the spur back and forth; there should be a little play. Modified mesh tends to have slightly less play than Stock or F1, to prevent stripping the spur gear with the greater torque.

End Bell Timing

You can increase the RPM of a brushless motor by advancing the motor timing. This is often done by loosening the end bell screws and rotating the end bell. You can see in the photo that the example motor is set to 20 degrees of end bell timing. To increase RPM increase the timing, e.g: to 25 degrees or more. Some notes of caution:

1. Increasing the end bell timing will increase your motor temperature (see Motor Temperature below).
2. Increasing end bell timing will reduce motor torque, i.e: the motor will have a faster top speed (RPM) but will accelerate slower (torque).

3. Never increase motor timing past the last timing mark by the manufacturer (in this case 50 degrees).
4. To increase motor timing, loosen (but don't remove) the black screws and rotate the end bell. In the case of our example motor, the silver screws hold the motor together. Most motors use a similar system for changing timing, although the colour of screws may vary.

Tuning Gearing for the Lowest Lap Times

Electric motors generate maximum torque at 1 RPM and the torque declines as the RPM increases. It is possible to lose too much low-end torque to effectively accelerate the weight of the car from a slow corner.

Track	Gearing	Result
Small, tight track	Smaller pinion	More torque, less top end RPM
Large, open track	Larger pinion	Less torque, higher top end RPM

Caution: changing gearing may affect Motor Temperature (see below).

Selecting the "best" gearing for a particular track is a compromise and often involves trial and error by changing the gearing and watching the lap times to see if they are faster or slower.

To accelerate this process when you race at a new track, ask other drivers that are using the same brand and model of motor for their FDR/Rollout recommendation.

Motor Temperature

Take the temperature of the motor using an infra-red temperature gauge. Some motors are more susceptible to heat than others, but as a rule of thumb, we want to make sure that our motor is 72°C (162°F) or less at the end of a race. If it is between 72°C and 80° C (176°F), then decrease the size of the pinion by 1 tooth or decrease the end bell timing by a couple of degrees. The motor can handle 80°C occasionally, but the motor life will not be as long as motors that operate at 72°C. If it is over 80°C then, unfortunately, the motor may have been damaged.

If it is under 65°C (149°F) at the end of the race, then you can risk lowering the FDR by increasing the size of the pinion by 1 tooth, or increasing the end bell timing by a couple of degrees.

Wait until your motor has cooled down and drive some more laps, this time stopping every 1 minute and taking the temperature.

Repeat the process until the car is as fast as you can make it while coming off the track at 72°C (162°F) or less.

If on race day the air temperature is hotter than when you carried out your testing, then consider raising the FDR or lowering the end bell timing so that you don't overheat the motor.

Overheating melts the solder inside the motor, and soon afterwards the motor will probably stop working. It might just go slowly, or it might grind to a halt in the middle of a race and start smoking! Motors that have overheated tend to smell (forever).

Tip: An alloy motor mount will assist in dissipating motor heat. As will a motor heat sink and/or fan.

Radio Settings

The following are general guidelines for use as a starting point.

1/12th Radio Settings

1/12th cars tend to have a lot of steering and you may wish to reduce it, particularly when starting out in the class. Recommendations include:

- **End Point Adjustment (EPA) Servo setting** – reducing the EPA to 70%–80% will reduce the amount of steering. As you get used to how much steering these cars have, you can increase this setting. Ideally, the EPA for left and right should be set to the same value so that handling to the left and right is equal. You can check the steering throw with your Toe gauge to ensure it is the same left to right.

- **Steering Curve (Expo)** – because the slightest input gives a lot of steering you can slow this down by using negative steering expo. -15% to -20% is a good starting point which will soften the initial steering input and allow the car to react gradually, without changing the total steering available.

Throttle Expo – In Stock leave this at zero. Modified drivers can use negative expo to mellow out the throttle input if there is low traction.

F1 Radio Settings

F1 cars tend to understeer. Braking before the corner reduces understeer. However, F1 cars are exceptionally sensitive to braking, and the smallest use of brakes can cause the car to spin. To eliminate this:

- **Brake End Point Adjustment (EPA)** – set the brake EPA to 80% as a starting point and increase or decrease as necessary.
- **ABS brakes** – If your radio has this setting, turn it on.

Note: at low speed, you may appear to have no brakes. That's normal. Brakes are needed when approaching a tight corner at high speed, and for that they should work fine.

You should now be able to brake by pumping the brakes, as you would in a real car to prevent lockups. Only ever brake in a straight line or the car will veer to one side. If you brake too hard the car will veer to one side or spin.

With the correct tyres for the track temperature and the correct Radio and ESC settings (refer page 61), you should now be able to brake going into corners without losing the back end.

Throttle Expo – It is important to gradually increase throttle in an F1 car, grabbing a handful of trigger is a sure way to end up in the wall. Use negative expo to mellow out the throttle input while not reducing the total throttle available. This has a similar effect to loosening the diff.

Ride Height

Overview

Ride height is measured with the wheels on the car and the car ready-to-race. When using rubber tyres, your ride height settings should stay fairly consistent, since rubber tyres do not lose significant diameter due to wear during use.

However, if using foam tyres, the car's ride height decreases as the foam tyres wear down to smaller diameters. Tyres may wear at different rates front-to-back, and left-to-right, which may eventually result in a car with uneven ride height at all four corners. For solutions to uneven wear refer to Tyres (page 91).

Setting	Effect
Decreasing Ride Height (lowering the car)	<ul><li>Faster steering response.</li><li>Reduces chassis roll.</li><li>Increases overall grip.</li><li>Better on smoother tracks.</li><li>Reduces likelihood of traction rolling.</li></ul>
Increasing Ride Height (raising the car)	<ul><li>Slower steering response.</li><li>Increases chassis roll.</li><li>Decreases overall grip.</li><li>Better on bumpy and asphalt tracks.</li><li>Increases likelihood of traction rolling.</li></ul>

Setting the front ride height to be lower than the rear by 0.5mm is a normal practice and provides:
- Increased corner entry steering.
- Increased stability in corners.
- Increased on-power oversteer and therefore reducing the difference between the front and rear ride heights will increase rear traction.

Measuring Ride Height

There are 5 locations to measure ride height, as shown in the following table and diagram:

Location	Measurement Location
Front	On the edge of the chassis plate at the front (left and right edges)
Middle	Where the side link connects to the rear pod (left and right edges)
Rear	At the centre of the rear pod plate

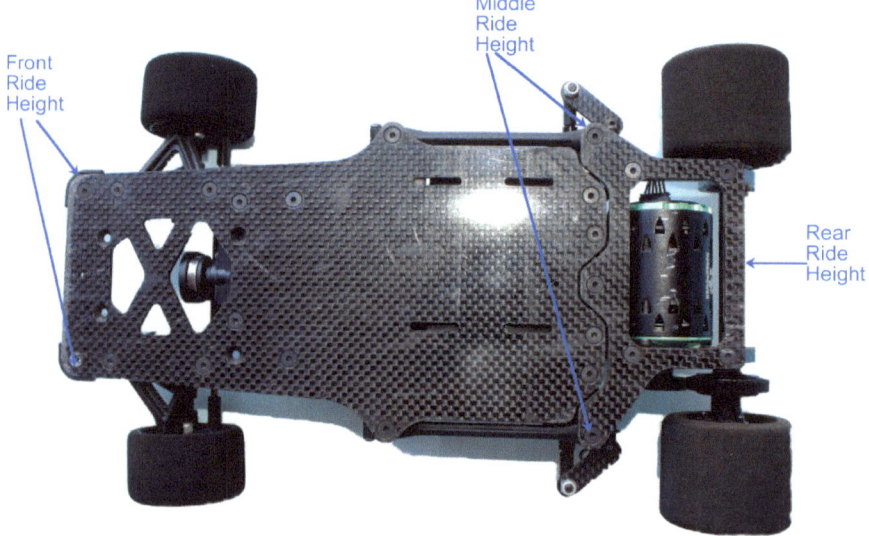

Note: F1 ride height should be measured just behind the front wing. Double-check the front wing does not droop and touch the track.

It is possible for the ride height on the left and right of the car to be different. This can cause issues, and is why we don't just measure in the centre of the front.

Possible causes:

- The left to right weight balance of the car may be different (refer page *94*).
- The car may be Tweaked (refer page *99*).
- The front ride height shims may not be the same on the left and the right side (they should be).
- The front springs may no longer rebound to the same length and therefore need replacing.
- The side springs may no longer rebound to the same length and therefore need replacing.
- The side springs pre-load may not be set correctly (refer page *82*).
- With foam tyres, the tyres may be different diameters left to right.

Starting Ride Height

The following are conservative starting ride heights:

Class	Track	Front	Middle	Rear
1/12th	Carpet	3.5mm	4mm	4mm
1/12th	Asphalt	4mm	4.5mm	4.5mm
F1	Carpet	4mm	4.5mm	4.5mm
F1	Asphalt	5mm	5.5mm	5.5mm

Important: Measure ride height when the car is race-ready, including battery.

Interactions

Recheck the ride height whenever you:
- Change tyres.
- Finish a run on foam tyres.
- Change Droop (refer page *75*) or Camber (refer page *44*).
- After a crash.

Ride Heights interact. As you increase the front ride height, the rear ride height will reduce slightly and vice versa. After changing one end of the car always re-check all five ride height measurements.

Front Ride Height

On most cars, front ride height can be changed by:
- Changing the shims above and below the steering block, or
- Changing the shims under the front lower bulkhead (the easiest option to adjust), or
- A combination of the above.

Shims must be the same on the left side as the right side of the car.

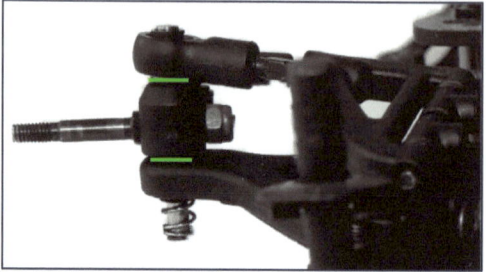

Shims above and below the steering block (shown in green).

Shims under the bulkhead (shown in red).

The following are a suggested starting point. The actual size of shims depends on the ride height you are trying to achieve.

Front Tyre Diameter	Shims on Kingpin (suggested starting point)	Shims Under Bulkhead (suggested starting point)
Small	1mm above steering block 0.6mm under steering block Total = 1.6mm *	0.5mm
Medium	1.5mm above steering block 0.1mm under steering block Total = 1.6mm *	1.5mm
Large	0.1mm above steering block 1.5mm under steering block Total = 1.6mm *	1.5mm

* Check your car's manual to determine the total width of shims. We have assumed 1.6mm in the above example. Always use the total specified in your car's manual or you may alter the Front Roll Centre (refer page 77). The reason for using a minimum of a 0.1mm shim, above and under the steering block, is to reduce the likelihood of binding.

To change front ride height:

Desired Ride Height Change	Shims Under Bulkhead **	Shims on Kingpin	Measurement Between Chassis and Axle
Increase	Decrease	Decrease the shims under the axle and increase the shims above the axle	Decreases

| Decrease | Increase | Increase the shims under the axle and decrease the shims above the axle | Increases |

** It is normally easier to adjust the shims under the bulkhead than on the kingpin.

Tyre Diameter Impact

With foam tyres, the ride height will reduce as the tyres wear. We recommend setting up your front ride height with, for example, 1.5mm of shims under the bulkhead and then reducing these shims as tyres wear to maintain the same ride height. The bulkhead shims are normally much quicker to change than the shims above and below the steering block.

Middle Ride Height

To adjust the Middle Ride Height, change the Centre Shock spring Preload. This is set by screwing the collar above the spring so that the spring is more compressed or less compressed.

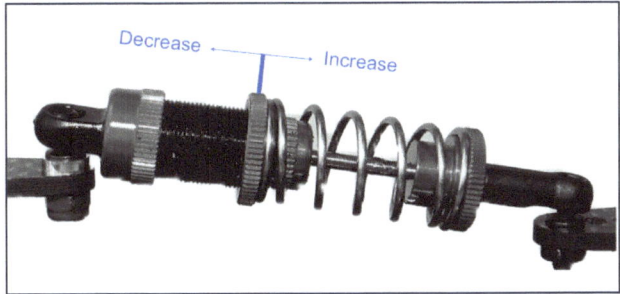

Preload Setting	Threaded Preload Collar	Middle Ride Height
Increase	Tighten collar so it compresses the spring	Increases
Decrease	Loosen the collar so it allows the spring to expand	Decreases

Changing the preload also affects the Rear Pod Droop (refer to page 58).

For more information on Centre Shock spring Preload (refer to page 54).

Rear Ride Height

To adjust rear ride height, some cars use bushings, and others use shims.

Bushings

Above: bushings on a plastic sprue
Left: 1mm bushing installed in the car

The hole in the bushing is offset by the number of millimetres written on the bushing. The bushing can be installed with the number to the top or the bottom.

The same offset number and orientation must be used on the left and the right of the car.

To change ride height:

Desired Ride Height Change	Bushings	Axle
Increase	• If offset number is currently oriented to the **top,** then increase the offset, *e.g: 1mm to 2mm increases ride height by 1mm.* • If offset number is currently oriented to the **bottom,** then decrease the offset, *e.g: 2mm to 1mm increases by 1mm*	Lowers
Decrease	• If offset number is currently oriented to the **top,** then decrease the offset, *e.g: 2mm to 1mm decreases the ride height by 1mm.* • If offset number is currently oriented to the **bottom,** then increase the offset, *e.g: 1mm to 2mm decreases ride height by 1mm.*	Raises

Initial setting:

Rear Tyre Diameter	Bushings
Small	Orient bushings so the offset number is at the **top** (which will offset the hole towards the bottom). The smaller the tyre, the more the hole is offset towards the bottom.
Medium	0 offset bushings (hole in middle of bushing).
Large	Orient bushings so the offset number is at the **bottom** (which will offset the hole towards the top). The larger the tyre, the more the hole is offset towards the top.

Make sure you use the same bushing on the left and the right and that it is offset in the same direction. A quick visual inspection should always show the axle to be parallel to the rear pod plate.

Shims

Shims are placed under the axle carrier (shown in green). The more shims used, the higher the axle, and the lower the ride height will be.

To change ride height:

Desired Ride Height Change	Shims	Measurement Between Rear Pod Plate and Axle
Increase	Reduce the thickness of shims	Decreases
Decrease	Increase the thickness of shims	Increases

Ride Height Interactions

When ride height is changed, the following may be affected and should be checked:

- Camber.
- Toe.
- Rear droop (when Middle and/or Rear Ride Height is changed). For instructions on changing Droop refer to page *58*.

When you do this to Ride Height	Also do this to Droop	Notes
Increase	Increase	Increasing ride height will decrease droop
Decrease	Decrease	Decreasing ride height will increase droop

Roll Bars

Refer to page *80*.

Roll Centre

The roll centre of the car is the imaginary point around which the car will roll when cornering. By adjusting the roll centre, we can make the car roll more or less and therefore increase or decrease the traction.

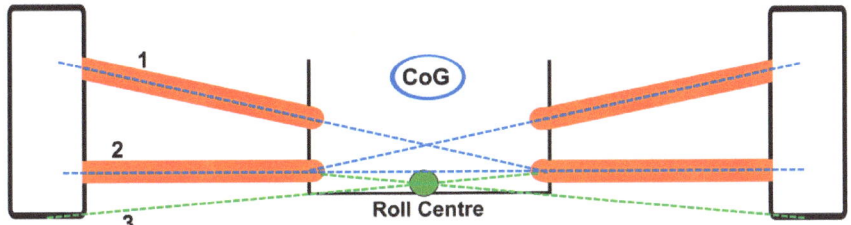

The illustration above shows the car from the front, including:
- The car's Centre of Gravity (CoG) (refer to page 94).
- The Roll Centre (green circle).

To calculate the front roll centre when the car is stationary:

1. Draw blue dotted line (1) through the top arm.
2. Draw blue dotted line (2) through the bottom arm.
3. Where lines (1) and (2) meet is an imaginary point called the Instant Centre.
4. Draw green dotted line (3) from the Instant Centre to the middle of the tyre contact patch.
5. Repeat for the other side of the car.
6. Where the two green dotted lines meet is the Roll Centre.

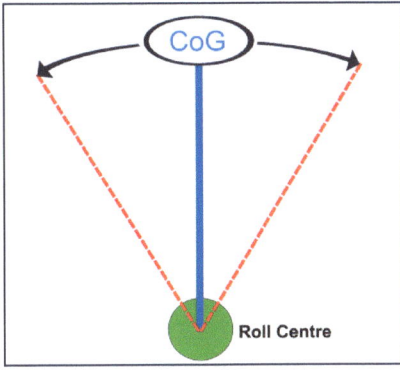

When cornering, the car will roll as shown in the diagram on the right, with the Centre of Gravity (CoG) rolling around the roll centre.

By raising the height of the roll centre, the blue line becomes shorter. The car will therefore not roll as much and traction will be reduced. It will take less time to roll so the car will react to steering inputs more quickly.

By lowering the height of the roll centre (above the track), the blue line becomes longer. Therefore, the car will roll more and traction will be increased. It will take more time to roll so the car will react slower to steering inputs.

Roll centre is a complex area of vehicle mechanics and has been simplified here. If you are reading other texts on roll centre, then you may find it helpful to know that it is the geometric roll centre described above (vehicle is stationary). When the suspension is compressed or lifted, the roll centre will move and the roll centre at any point in time is called the instantaneous roll centre. How much the roll centre moves when the suspension compresses is determined by the relative angle between the top and bottom arms, and the arm length.

The front suspension has a different roll centre to the rear suspension, and these are described separately below.

Front Roll Centre

The front roll centre is determined by the relative angle between the upper and lower arms (also called A-arms or wishbones). Most pan cars have fixed lower arms, so that angle can't be changed. Therefore to control front roll centre, we change the angle of the upper arm (marked as "1" on the diagram on the previous page):

Lower/ Raise	How to Change	Effect
To lower front roll centre (increase amount of roll)	Make the front suspension arms more horizontal (parallel to the track) by increasing shims under the arm hinge-pin	<ul><li>More on-throttle steering during mid-corner and corner exit.</li><li>Increases front traction mid-corner and corner exit.</li><li>Car is slower to respond.</li><li>Better on smooth, high grip tracks with fast corners.</li></ul>
To raise front roll centre (decrease amount of roll)	Make the suspension arms more angled by decreasing shims under the arm hinge-pin	<ul><li>Less on-throttle steering during mid-corner and corner exit.</li><li>Decreases front traction mid-corner and corner exit.</li><li>Car is quicker to respond.</li><li>Use in high grip conditions to avoid traction rolling.</li><li>Use on tracks with quick direction changes (chicanes).</li></ul>

Note: We assume you change the shims under the hinge-pin, (i.e: on the end of the suspension arm closest to the centre of the car) because a number of kits have this option. If your car has other options such as changing shims at the end of the top suspension arm closest to the wheel, or changing the angle of the lower arm, then refer to the diagram on page 75 to determine whether this lowers or raises the roll centre.

Interaction

Lowering the roll centre by increasing the angle of the upper front arm will slightly increase the Camber Gain (refer to page 46). However, it will probably not be noticeable.

Rear Roll Centre

The rear roll centre is determined by the interaction between the centre pivot and the side links. It is changed by adding or reducing shims under the Side Links (refer to page 78).

Rollout

Refer to *Gearing & Rollout* on page 61.

Shock Absorber

Refer to Damping on page 50.

Side Links (to rear pod)

It is important that the side links move smoothly on their balls without binding and without significant play. If a side link doesn't move smoothly, back off the screw holding the side links on the ball. If there is significant play, then replace.

Adding shims under the side link balls changes the rear roll centre (refer page 78):

Change	Roll Centre	Effect
Increase shims	Raises	<ul><li>Increases steering.</li><li>Reduces rear traction.</li></ul>
Decreases shims	Lowers	<ul><li>Reduces steering.</li><li>Increases rear traction.</li></ul>

Some cars have optional holes for the connection of the side links between the main chassis and rear pod. Optional holes are normally at the front of the car with the outermost hole keeping the side link parallel with each other and the innermost hole angling the front of the side link towards the centre of the car:

Change	Effect
Inner hole (closer to chassis)	More mid-corner steering, more aggressive feel
Outer hole (further from chassis)	More neutral handling, more linear cornering feel

Ensure that the side links on each side of the car use the same holes (inner or outer holes, left and right).

Springs

The springs determine the amount of chassis roll, as well as how quickly the chassis rolls.

If the car is rolling significantly, it will create a great deal of grip due to more weight being transferred onto the outside tyres in the turn. This is good for low grip tracks. But on high grip tracks, this will decrease the corner speed and slow the "change of direction" responsiveness.

When do you know whether you have the best spring tension combination? Refer to the table below:

	Springs Too Soft	"Best" Spring Rate	Springs Too Hard/Stiff
Low Grip Track	This situation is the hardest to identify. Car will be slower in the corners that it could be.	Springs soft enough to generate sufficient grip without unduly slowing the car.	Car will grip initially, but part way into a corner, well before the apex, the rear end will break away suddenly and substantially.
High Grip Track	Decreases the corner speed and slows the 'change of direction' responsiveness.	Harder springs while still generating sufficient grip without unduly slowing the car.	Car 'hops' or 'chatters' across the track when cornering.

In order to minimise lap times, aim to limit the chassis roll as much as possible by using harder springs without the car chattering or the rear end breaking away unexpectedly. Of course, you still need sufficient rear grip to accelerate as early as possible out of the corners, and sufficient front grip to generate the steering you want. As with all car setup, it is about finding the best balance for your driving style at the current track.

Roll Bars

Some cars have the option of Roll Bars, also called Anti-Roll Bars, Torsion Bars or Sway Bars.

Roll bars can be used to limit the chassis roll while running slightly softer springs than would otherwise be possible, giving more steering going into a corner, more rear grip coming out of the corner and better stability and directional responsiveness.

Centre Shock Spring

Refer to page 53.

Front Springs & Lube

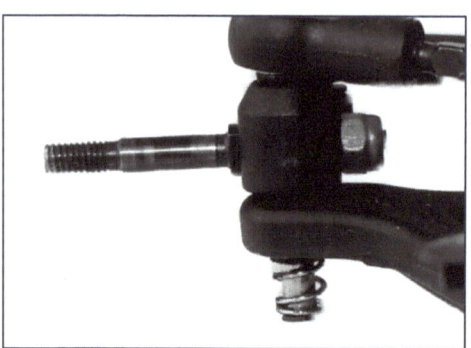

Front Spring	Effect
Softer	• More overall steering. • Better on bumpy tracks. • Has a higher chance of collapsing under load.
Harder	• Less overall steering. • Better on smooth tracks. • Easier to drive and smoother in the corners. • Increases the chance of traction rolling.

Use the same front spring on the left and the right side.

Front Kingpin Lubrication

Track	Lubrication
Low traction or bumpy tracks	10k cSt
High traction or smooth tracks	30k cSt

Use the same lubrication on the left and the right side. Re-lubricate the kingpins at the start of each race day.

Side Springs

Side Springs	Effect
Softer	- Less overall steering. - The car will roll more but will be less likely to traction roll.
Harder	- More responsive with a quicker direction change. - More difficult to drive.

Setting Side Spring Preload (Coin Trick)

This setting adjusts Tweak (refer to page 98).

It is important that the springs are contacting the chassis with the correct amount of force. Otherwise, the chassis may not be parallel to the ground nor return to this position quickly and correctly after cornering.

Setting the Side Spring Preload using the Coin Trick:

1. Remove side dampers.

2. Unscrew the side spring grub screws until the side springs are just touching the chassis.

3. With tyres on, settle the car on its suspension by tapping it down. Note: it is important that the front left and right tyres are the same diameter, and the rear left and right tyres are the same diameter.

4. Take two coins of the same denomination (larger coins make the test more sensitive and are recommended). Place one coin on each of the left and right front tyres over the axle.

5. Lift the front of the car slowly with a driver (or finger) under the centre of the chassis. The suspension will unload, and when the front tyres lift off the ground, the coins will fall. Both coins should fall simultaneously.

6. If one coin falls before the other one, then you need to adjust the side spring that is diagonally opposite, i.e: if the coin on the front left tyre drops first then you need to tighten the right-hand side spring. Note: If you need to tighten by more than ½ a turn total then either step 2 above was not carried out correctly or your car may be tweaked (refer page 99).

7. Repeat steps 3–6 until both tyres leave the ground at the same time.

8. Re-connect side dampers. Hold the car in one hand by the main chassis only. Twist the rear pod to simulate the car rolling to the left. The chassis should immediately move off the spring, (i.e: the chassis and spring are no longer touching). If it doesn't then you have introduced too much preload in step 6 above and the car will be more sensitive/twitchy than with correct preload. Repeat this step with the car rolling to the right.

Steering Arm Ball-cup Location

Refer to *Ackermann* on page *41*.

Steering Linkage Angle

The thickness of the shims under the steering arm ball determines the angle of the steering linkage compared to the chassis. The linkages are often angled so they are higher at the wheel end than at the centre of the chassis.

When the car goes over a bump, the steering angle may be affected. This is called "bump steer". The car is more susceptible to bump steer when the steering linkage turnbuckle is parallel to the track.

Shims	Steering Linkage Angle	Effect
Less Shims	Smaller angle, closer to parallel to the track	• Increased in-corner steering. • Car harder to drive. • Better for smooth track. • More susceptible to bump steer.
More Shims	Greater angle, less parallel to the track	• Decreased in-corner steering. • Car easier to drive. • Better for bumpy track. • Less susceptible to bump steer.

The steering linkage angle can often be changed on the end of the steering linkage closest to the centre of the car. The photo to the right shows two options; green provides a greater steering linkage angle while the red hole makes it more parallel to the track.

Another setting for changing the steering feel is *Ackermann* on page *41*.

T-Bar

A T-Bar was common in older 1/12th and F1 cars to connect the rear pod to the main chassis. This was largely replaced by the pivot-ball link rear suspension. However, it is still available on the following cars at the time of writing:

Tamiya F104 Pro II

This chassis uses a rear pod with integrated T-Bar. It does not have side links or side springs.

T-Bar	Friction Damper
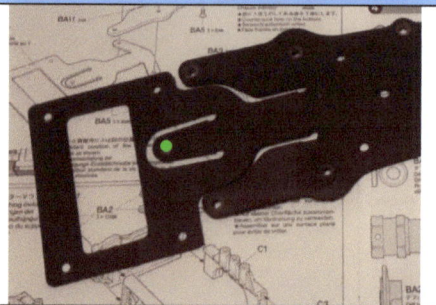	
Centre Adjustment Screw (green): This controls chassis roll from side to side. The best setting will vary depending on the track surface and traction available. A good starting point is to back off the screw so there is no compression of the o-ring. Then tighten until you feel the o-ring starting to compress. Then back off the screw half a turn. From that starting point: • Looser = increases rear traction, reduces steering response (good for low traction track) • Tighter = reduces rear traction, increase steering response (good for high traction track) Caution: when loosening the screw ensure it doesn't scrape the track surface or fall out (use Loctite or a locknut as necessary).	**Adjustment Nut (blue alloy):** This provides 360 degree damping of the rear pod and can be used for fine-tuning once you have set the side roll with the T-Bar Centre Adjustment Screw, and the weight transfer front to rear with the Centre Shock. • Looser = maximises movement already set. • Tighter = further restricts movement already set. On a car struggling for rear grip unscrew the nut completely.

Car Setup Reference

Using the Coin Trick with a T-Bar

This setting adjusts Tweak (refer to page *98*).

To ensure the weight on the front tyres is equal, you can use the coin trick as follows:

1. With tyres on, settle the car on its suspension by tapping it down. Note: it is important that the front left and right tyres are the same diameter, and the rear left and right tyres are the same diameter.

2. Take two coins of the same denomination (larger coins make the test more sensitive and are recommended). Place one coin on each of the left and right front tyres over the axle.

3. Lift the front of the car slowly with a driver (or finger) under the centre of the chassis. The suspension will unload, and when the front tyres lift off the ground, the coins will fall. Both coins should fall simultaneously.

4. If one coin falls before the other one, then you need to adjust the T-Bar screw that is diagonally opposite as follows:

Wheel	Issue	Solution
Front left lifts first	The rear left tyre has too much weight on it	• Loosen right T-bar screw by $1/8^{th}$ of a turn, and • Tighten left T-bar screw by $1/8^{th}$ of a turn, then • Re-check and repeat as necessary
Front right lifts first	The rear right tyre has too much weight on it	• Loosen left T-bar screw by $1/8^{th}$ of a turn, and • Tighten right T-bar screw by $1/8^{th}$ of a turn, then • Re-check and repeat as necessary

5. Repeat steps 1–4 and adjust until both tyres leave the ground at the same time. If you need to tighten/loosen screws by a significant amount then your car may be tweaked (refer page *99*).

Tamiya TRF103

As an option you can replace the rear pod, side links and side springs, with a T-bar. Tamiya recommends the T-bar for extremely low traction surfaces.

When a T-bar is installed refer to the F104 Pro II above for:
- Centre Adjustment Screw settings, and
- Using the Coin Trick with a T-Bar.

Toe

Toe-out is when the front of the wheel points away from the centreline of the car. Conversely, toe-in is when the front of the wheel points in towards the centreline of the car.

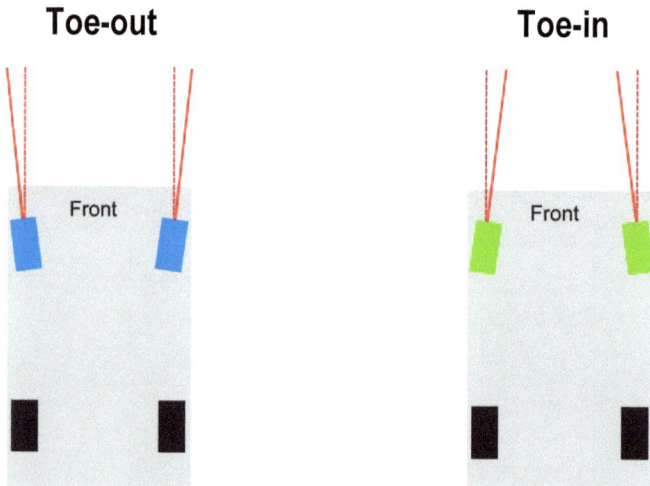

Front toe angle

Front Toe	Effect
Toe-out	Increases straight line stability and decreases the chance of the car wandering in a straight line. Provides more corner entry steering.
Toe-in	Gives more mid-exit steering but makes the car more difficult to drive, particularly in a straight line.

1–1.5° Toe-out is a good starting point.

Front toe-out works differently on a rear wheel drive compared to a 4WD. Because there is no drive to the front wheels adding toe-out makes the car much more stable in a straight line.

Increasing the front toe angle (in or out) will result in decreased straight line speed (although less of an issue in the Modified class).

Rear toe angle

Most pan cars do not have adjustable rear toe.

In general, the more rear toe-in, the more stable your car will be. The rear wheels of your race car should always be adjusted with some degree of toe-in. Rear toe-out is never used.

Increasing the angle of rear toe-in will result in decreased straight line speed but the car will be more stable.

Track Width

Most racing classes will have rules specifying the maximum track width.

Front Track Width

Front track width is adjusted by adding/removing shims to the front wheel axles between the hubs and the wheel. It is critical to use the same thickness of shims on both left and right sides.

Front Track Width	Effect
Wider (more shims)	• Decreases front grip. • Slower steering response. • Increases understeer.
Narrower (less shims)	• Increases front grip. • Faster steering response. • Decreases understeer.

Interaction

Changing the front track-width setting will not change the front toe setting if shims are used as shown. However, if your car uses shims/bushings on the suspension arms (or anywhere inboard of the steering arms), then toe will be affected.

Rear Track Width

Rear track width is adjusted by adding/removing shims on the rear axle between the bearings and the hubs. It is critical to use the same thickness of shims on both left and right sides. There must always be a small amount of play in the axle (side-to-side) to ensure it rotates freely and does not bind.

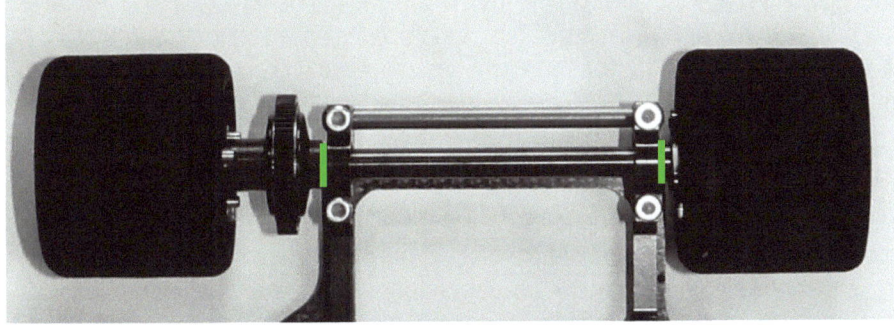

Rear Track Width	Effect
Wider (more shims)	• Increases car stability. • Increases rear grip at corner entry and mid corner. • Decreases cornering speed.
Narrower (less shims)	• Increases car responsiveness. • Increases rear grip at corner exit. • Increases cornering speed. • Increases on-power steering.

Tyres & Additives

The correct tyre choice is critical to your setup. Most major races will specify control tyres so that all racers are on an even playing field. However, if you have the choice of tyres then ask the local fast drivers what they are using.

This section is not a guide to tyre selection; rather, it provides information on getting the most from the tyres you use.

As a general rule, the softer the tyres are, the more grip they will provide. You may run a different tyre compound on the front of the car compared to the rear. Running softer tyres on the rear will improve rear-end traction, while softer tyres at the front will increase steering – the softer the tyre, the greater the likelihood of overheating on a hot track.

Rubber Tyres

When using rubber tyres, your ride height settings should stay consistent, since rubber tyres do not reduce in diameter significantly from run to run (although rears will see more wear than fronts). The wear on rubber tyres affects grip but does not normally cause the issues listed for foam below.

Rubber tyres are more likely to come unglued from the wheels than foam and should be checked after each run and re-glued if necessary.

Rubber tyres on outside asphalt are more susceptible to track temperature changes than rubber tyres on carpet, or foam tyres on any surface.

For examples of Rubber Tyre usage refer to the Case Studies chapter beginning on page *105*.

Foam Tyres

Tyre warmers are not required with foam tyres. However, on low grip surfaces, they may assist the traction additive to soften the tyres and therefore generate additional grip.

Foam tyres are not as susceptible to track temperature changes as rubber tyres.

As foam tyres wear, the reduction in diameter means you should check after each run:

- **Ride Height** (refer to page *68*) – The car's ride height decreases as the foam tyres wear down to smaller diameters. Tyres may wear at different rates front-to-back and left-to-right, because the track may have more corners, or high-speed corners, in one direction. This may lead to a car with uneven ride height at all four corners. If necessary, swap tyres left to right to maintain even wear. Some racers will true tyres to maintain even ride height.
- **Gearing** (refer to Rollout on page *63*).
- **Tyre Coning** i.e: either the inside or outside of the tyre is wearing at a faster rate causing the tyre to "cone". Check Camber and adjust as necessary to promote even wear across the surface of the tyre and prevent coning (refer page *44*).

Check after each run that tyres remain firmly glued to the rims and re-glue if necessary.

For examples of Foam Tyre usage refer to the Case Studies chapter beginning on page *105*.

Truing 1/12th Tyres

It is common to use a tyre truer to shave foam from 1/12th tyres to provide appropriate grip and handling for the surface.

There are a number of factors which influence tyre diameter (including budget, race event and tyre compound), so this is a general guide only.

In this example, we assume that a new set of foam rear tyres has a diameter of 46mm. The following are suggested starting points:

Rear Diameter	Surface	Comments
46mm	Asphalt	Leave tyres untrued, as taller side walls provide more flex and therefore more grip. While this will work on carpet it may provide too much traction and therefore reduce steering and speed
42mm	Carpet	Medium grip
40mm	Carpet	High grip

True front tyres to be 1–1.5mm smaller than the rears.

Additive

Additive softens the tyre and increases grip. Normally a track's grip will increase during the race meeting as rubber and additive are laid down on the track and track temperature increases. This may mean reducing the application of additive as the meeting goes on to maintain the level of grip for which you have set up your car.

Additive is normally applied some time before the race and allowed to soak into the tyres, softening the rubber or foam. How long before depends on the tyre compound, the additive, the track surface and temperature, air temperature and whether tyre warmers are used. However, leaving the additive on for at least 15 minutes is a good starting point. Manufacturers produce different additive products for rubber and foam tyres.

For pan cars it is normal to always apply additive across the entire surface of the rear tyres and to some or all of the front tyres, depending on how much steering is needed. If applying additive only to a portion of the front tyre, then always start at the inside of the tyre (the part closest to the chassis) as this part of the tyre should be touching the track before the car starts to turn (assuming negative Camber, refer page 44) and should continue to touch the track throughout the turn. Whereas the outside of the tyre might only touch the track close to the corner apex.

For examples of additive usage, refer to the Case Studies chapter beginning on page 105.

Tyre Warmers

Tyre warmers have two primary uses:

1. Warm rubber tyres to their operating temperature so that they provide good grip as soon as the car is placed on the track. If you do not use tyre warmers, then you will need to do some warm-up laps to heat the tyres before the race. Foam tyres do not normally require warming.

2. To improve the absorption of additive. By heating the tyre while the additive is absorbed, the additive should soften the tyre to a greater degree than without tyre warmers.

For examples of tyre warmer usage refer to the Case Studies chapter beginning on page 105.

Weight

Most racing classes have a minimum weight rule where the race-ready car must be at least that weight. Depending on your car, battery, motor and electronics choices, this may mean it is necessary to add weight, or you may be looking for ways to reduce weight.

A heavy car will usually have more traction than a lighter car. However, a lighter car will be faster than a heavy car. Because our goal is the fastest possible lap-time, we normally run the car as close to the minimum weight as possible and change the setup of the car to provide the traction needed.

It can be risky to run too close to the weight limit as cars found to be below the weight limit after the race may be disqualified. Foam tyre wear may reduce the weight of the car slightly.

If you need to add weight, then do so as low on the chassis as possible and check that the car remains balanced left to right. Both of these are explained below.

Centre of Gravity

The Centre of Gravity (CoG) of the car is the balance point of the mass of the car. The lower the CoG, the better. This is achieved by placing all electronics as low as possible on the chassis and minimising any weight that is high up.

The higher the CoG, the more the car will roll in a corner. It is better to keep the CoG as low as possible and change the Roll Centre to increase chassis roll if required (refer to page 76).

Weight Balance (Side to Side)

You should always try to adjust the weight on your main chassis, so it is equal left to right. This will assist with consistent handling, and with ride height which is similar on both sides of the chassis. It is easiest to do this while building the kit and should be done without the rear pod connected.

It is not normal to balance the rear pod left to right although it can be done if you wish.

Pan cars are not normally balanced front to back.

Manufacturers will often provide a hole in the chassis at the front and rear of the car to check side to side weight balance. Imagine two nails sticking up from your pit table and the car balancing on these nails (one nail per hole in the chassis). You can buy a tool for this or make your own.

Make sure your pit board is perfectly flat and check this with a spirit level. Otherwise, the weight balance reading might not be accurate.

The ESC is normally the heaviest item so the receiver and transponder can be placed on the opposite side of the chassis from the ESC. If your car leans to one side then move the electronics so that the car sits level.

A number of manufacturers will allow:
- The servo, and/or
- The battery

to be shifted to the right or left side of the car to assist with weight balance.

Due to their construction, lipo batteries may be slightly lighter on the plug end so put this on the side of the car with the ESC.

A small amount of lead weight can be added to one side to balance the car if required. However, this is not ideal as we want the car to be as light as possible, provided it meets the class's minimum weight rule.

Moving Weight (Front to Rear)

Re-distributing existing weight can be a useful tuning tool. This is most easily done by moving the battery location (refer to page *43*).

Adding Weight to Increase Steering or Rear Traction

Car handling is determined by weight transfer (refer to page 21). However, the car should be kept as close to the minimum class weight as possible. Adding weight to the front for more steering or the rear pod to increase rear grip is not normally a good idea and may even provide the opposite result of what is intended. This is because it is the transfer of weight to one end of the car that changes car handling.

If you take any car and double its weight, then it will not be able to take the corner as quickly because it must change the direction of the additional weight. Adding physical weight to the rear of the car to correct oversteer could make the car oversteer even more because the car must now change the direction of this extra weight when cornering. As a general rule, the lighter your car, the better it will corner.

Although static weight certainly impacts handling, it should only be added in extremely slippery conditions such as a wet or extremely low grip track (in which case add it to the centre of the main chassis as low down as possible). When adding static weight, make sure your car remains balanced left to right (as above), and add the weight as low down as possible.

To increase steering without adding weight, refer to the checklist on page 149.

To increase rear traction without adding weight, refer to the checklist on page 147.

If after reading this you still want to add weight at one end of the car, then I recommend no more than 10–15g (.02–.03 pounds).

Wheelbase

Wheelbase is the distance between the front and rear axle. The greater the distance, the longer the wheelbase, the shorter the distance, the shorter the wheelbase. Some cars have the option of changing the wheelbase:

Wheelbase	Effect
Longer (green in example photo)	• Better for larger tracks. • Better for longer corners (sweepers).
Shorter (red in example photo)	• Better for tight technical tracks. • Better for tracks with many 180 degree corners. • The car rotates better in the centre of the corner. • Car carries more corner speed.

Wings

1/12th

For 1/12th Bodies refer to page *43*.

F1

Front Wing

The front wing affects the aerodynamic downforce on the front tyres. Selecting a wing with greater downforce will increase steering and reduce straight-line speed slightly. Because this is an aerodynamic effect, the faster the car enters the corner, the more steering the front wing will provide.

Rear Wing

The rear wing affects the aerodynamic downforce on the rear tyres. Selecting a wing with greater downforce will increase rear-end grip and reduce straight-line speed slightly. Because this is an aerodynamic effect, the faster the car enters the corner, the more rear-end grip the rear wing will provide.

Some manufacturers offer a choice of mounting locations for the rear wing. The higher the wing is mounted, the greater the downforce generated and the greater the impact on straight-line speed.

Chapter 4

Tweak

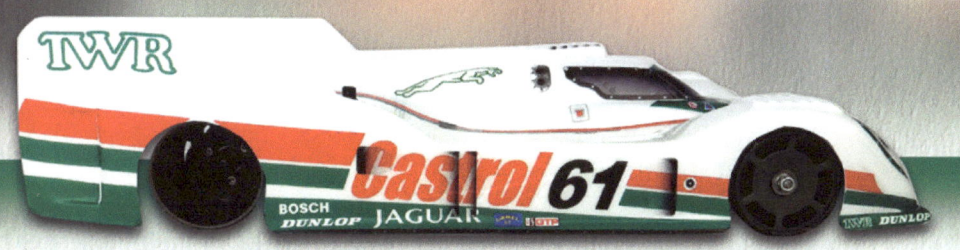

What is Tweak?

Tweak is the adjustment of the suspension so that both rear tyres touch the ground with equal pressure, and both front tyres touch the ground with equal pressure.

To set Tweak, refer to Setting Side Spring Preload (Coin Trick) on page 82 (or if you have a T-Bar car then page 86). Alternatively, you can purchase a Tweak Station (making sure that it has been designed for pan cars).

If after setting the Tweak above, one side still has more pressure than the other then the car is "tweaked".

A "tweaked" car displays inconsistent handling. In particular, if it turns to one side when accelerating in a straight line.

A "tweaked" car may have:

- A twisted main chassis.
- A twisted rear pod.

The main chassis and rear pod are the central attachment points for all suspension components, and if one or both are twisted it will unbalance all suspension settings. This may occur as the result of a crash. Provided the twisting is not a result of physical damage to the car, then it can be corrected by following the steps in this chapter.

Quick Checks

1. With the car race-ready but body off, turn the car over and hold the main chassis in your hand without holding the rear pod. Use a straight edge such as a steel ruler to check:

    a. The main chassis appears flat. Check from front to back and also diagonally from the front left of the main chassis to the rear right, and front right to rear left (if not flat, refer to Main Chassis heading below).

    b. The rear pod appears flat. Check diagonally from the front left of the rear pod to the rear right, and front right to rear left (if not flat, refer to Rear Pod heading below).

    c. The rear pod and main chassis are flat relative to each other, i.e: the straight edge continues over both the main chassis and rear pod in a straight line with no gaps under the ruler (if not, you may have positive rear droop, refer to page 58).

2. Put down the straight edge and twist the rear pod slightly one way to simulate cornering. When you let the rear pod go, it should return to being in the same plane as the main chassis. Now twist the other way and let go. If the rear pod does not return to the same plane as the main chassis, in either direction, then refer to Setting Side Spring Preload (Coin Trick) on page 82 (or if you have a T-Bar car page 86).

Rear Pod

The rear pod must move freely side to side and up and down. There are three things you should check:

1. **Body Should Not Cause Binding** – When the body is fitted movement of the rear pod must not be hindered by the body or the motor wires. Sometimes the motor wires will be fine when the body is off, but the body may push them against the car when fitted. Use 16 AWG gauge wire for 12th Stock and F1. Use 12 AWG for Modified. It is less risky to put the wires over the top of the chassis mounting plates, rather than under the side damper tubes. However, if there is plenty of room and no risk of binding, then it can be tidier to run wires underneath the side dampers.

Make sure the body doesn't press the wires into the chassis (causing binding).

2. **Rear Pod Should Remain True** – In a hard hit the weight of the motor can tweak the rear pod:

   a. Place a straight edge, such as a steel ruler, against the bottom of the rear pod from the front left corner to the rear right corner. The ruler should be flush against the bottom of the pod. Repeat for the opposite corners.

   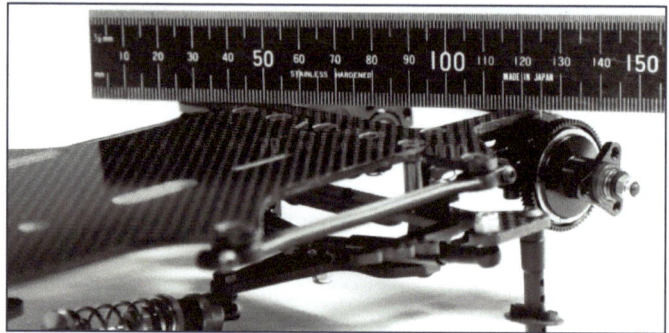

   b. If the ruler is not flush against the bottom of the pod, then the pod is tweaked:

      i. Loosen all of the screws under the rear pod slightly (say half a turn) i.e: screws mounting the bulkheads or uprights. This should remove the tension causing the tweak.

      ii. Gently tighten the screws using the following pattern:

      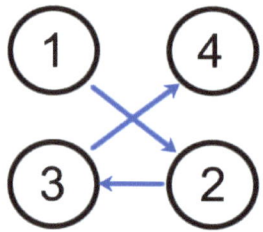

      iii. Re-check with a ruler (step a above). If the pod is still tweaked then:

         (1) Take the motor out of the car and remove the rear pod from the main chassis.

(2) Place the rear pod on a flat surface and press down on the corners of the pod. It will probably rock backwards and forwards when it should be flat. This causes uneven pressure on the rear wheels.

(3) Take the rear pod apart and check each part is straight and hasn't been bent or damaged. Replace any damaged parts and re-assemble. Pod should now sit flat and not rock when tested on a flat surface.

(4) Re-assemble and re-check with a ruler (step a above).

3. **Centre Pivot-ball Should Move Freely** – Remove the wheels, disconnect the centre shock, and disconnect the side dampers. The rear pod should move completely freely and smoothly in all directions; up, down, left and right. If it doesn't move freely in all directions or if you hear a clicking sound then there's an issue:

　　a. Unscrew the two screws that hold the rear pod to the main chassis.
　　b. The pod should now move completely freely without clicking.
　　c. Re-tighten the two screws, a little at a time, alternating sides until tight.
　　d. Re-check. Pod should move freely without clicking. If the problem persists, then check the balls the side links rest on and the centre pivot-ball. One of these is probably binding.

Main Chassis

Test for Tweak

Components that are screwed to the main chassis might move in a crash and cause the car to be tweaked:

Method 1 – Quick Test

Place a straight edge, such as a steel ruler, against the bottom of the chassis from the front left corner to the rear right corner. The ruler should be flush against the bottom of the chassis. Repeat for the opposite corners. If the ruler is not flush against the bottom of the chassis, then it is tweaked:

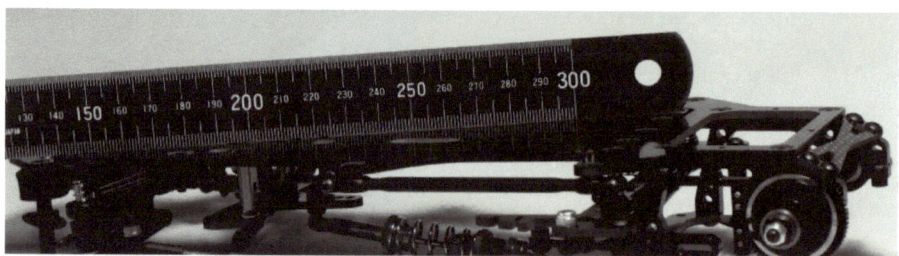

Method 2 – Detailed Test

1. Take off the wheels and place the car on a surface which is known to be perfectly flat, a pit setup board or sheet of glass is ideal. If using a pit table or other surface which should be flat then check it first with a steel ruler. If any gaps show between the ruler and the surface, then it is not perfectly flat.

2. Push down on opposite corners of the chassis and see if it rocks (front left and rear right, next try front right and rear left). The car should be perfectly flat on the surface, if it rocks then double-check that the chassis isn't rocking on something like a protruding screw head or battery tape. If the chassis is flat on the surface but it still rocks, then the main chassis is tweaked.

Chassis Tweaked Solution

If the main chassis is tweaked then one or more of the components attached to the chassis may have moved:

1. Loosen all of the screws under the main chassis slightly (say half a turn) i.e: screws mounting the servo, front suspension arms, T-bar (if you have one), any chassis bulkheads or uprights. This should remove the tension causing the tweak.

2. Gently tighten the screws using the following pattern:

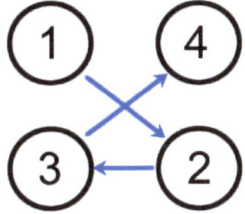

3. Before fully tightening the screws, re-check the chassis to see if it sits flat.

    a. If it sits flat, then proceed to step d below.

    b. If it doesn't sit flat then there may be components secured to the main chassis from the top which are tweaked, therefore:
        i. Loosen those screws and re-loosen the screws under the chassis.
        ii. Gently tighten them all using the pattern in step 2 above.
        iii. Re-check the chassis to see if it sits flat. If it does, proceed to step d below.

    c. Sometimes the servo can twist slightly. Loosen the screws holding the servo in place and see if the chassis now sits flat. If it does, proceed to step d.

    d. Fully tighten the screws using the pattern in step 2 above. Re-check the chassis to see if it sits flat. If it does, then you have removed the tweak from your chassis. If it doesn't then possibilities include: you have over-tightened screws, or tightened them in the wrong order, or a bulkhead or other component has been bent or damaged.

Chapter 5
Case Studies

Case Studies 5

This chapter describes actual race meetings and how skilled drivers approached their setup, what changes they made, why, and how car performance improved.

Different cars have unique handling characteristics. Even with the same chassis, driver style varies. That is why it is not recommended that you copy a world champion's car setup without understanding the settings. Instead, identify the differences between the world champion's setup and your car's setup and make one change at a time. Determine whether your car handles better or worse, based on your skill level and driving style, and fine-tune from there.

Carpet Case Studies

Starting Setup

If you have not raced at a particular track before, then we recommend starting with your chassis manufacturer's base carpet setup. You may also wish to search your chassis manufacturer's website for another driver's setup at that track so that you can note changes they made. We do not recommend using another driver's setup without knowing why they made the changes they did. However, it can be very useful to note the differences to the manufacturer's base carpet setup and then try each change, one at a time, and note whether it feels better or worse.

Changes Compared to Asphalt

1. Carpet tracks tend to be much smoother than asphalt and therefore you should set the ride height as low as possible. Check the minimum ride height allowed by the scrutineers. Make sure chassis screws are not protruding, as they might catch on the carpet.
2. Carpet generally provides more grip, and is less bumpy, than an asphalt track. The car can, therefore, be much stiffer while still providing sufficient grip. Refer to page *80* for how stiff you should make your car.
3. Tyre wear on carpet is significantly less than on asphalt.
4. Normally indoor tracks will have similar track temperatures throughout the day.

1/12th

First Case Study Track

Chesterfield Shootout Series, UK. Flat, medium grip, high speed.

Track Temperature

20–22°C

Control Tyre

Tyres were open for this event and, as the carpet was Grey Prima, I used JFT Pink rears and Magenta fronts all day. Tyre wear is usually quite acceptable at 0.2–0.3mm a run, so small tyres for additional corner speed and ease of driving were used.

I try and only use tyres once a day, but sometimes if you use them twice a day they start faster on the second run. This was the case at this event.

Control Additive

Additive was open. I used Spider Blue.

The Race Meeting

Car 1: Roche P12 Evo Chassis – 1st in Stock – David Spashett

Modified was not run at this meeting, so I ran in Stock. I qualified 2nd behind Ollie Payne and finished first overall.

I kept the tyre prep simple for round 1 and applied Spider blue for 40mins on the rear and 10mins on the front. During the run, the grip did change, and the balance went more to the front, so right away, I knew I needed to make some changes.

Case Studies

Round 2 I applied the rear additive in the same way (entire tyre width) but on the front I used a lot less (inside half) but for a longer time, and this helped keep the same balance front to rear. Now happy with the tyre prep, I could look at car setup.

I was losing out on the high-speed corners due to a little initial rear-end slide. I decided to make a small change to the rear of the car. Stiffer side springs and thinner oil (reduced from 20K to 10K) gave a much better balance and allowed me to push harder.

With the natural evolution of the track it was difficult to quantify setup changes for speed, but in regards to balance changes my final setup change was to move the lipo forward, increasing high-speed steering and reducing low-speed steering a little. A couple of extra clicks of steering EPA increased the steering lock and the car felt stable and consistent for the full 8 minutes and gave me a car I could change line and control through the run.

When going to an event, I never look to find a completely new and revolutionary setup, but work with my base setup from the previous event and fine-tune things to help give me what I need to be comfortable and race. I am always of the opinion that, on these shorter one-day events, you are better to learn to drive an 85% car at 100% than try and find a 100% setup that you never learn to drive and make mistakes trying to get there.

- Ride height: front 3.4mm, middle 3.4mm, rear 3.6mm.
- Rear droop: 1mm.
- Long wheelbase +1mm.
- Caster 3.25°.
- Reactive Caster 5°.
- Shock oil 40Wt, 50% rebound, 2 hole piston, hard spring.
- Ball Diff setting: tight.
- Side Damper: 10K oil, long position.
- Side springs: hard.
- Front springs: medium.
- Front Toe-out: 0.5°
- Width: front 167.5mm, rear 171.5mm.
- Aluminium chassis.
- Forward battery position.
- Short side link.
- Tyre diameters: front 40.5mm, rear 41mm.
- Weight: 730g.
- Body: BA-06.
- Rollout: 71mm.

Second Case Study Track

RCRA Australian Indoor On-road Championships, EPiC Track, Canberra, Australia. CRC Carpet (bumpy in places). High grip. Technical track.

Track Temperature

Track temperature varied between 15°C (59°F) in the early morning to 20°C (68°F) later in the day. Change in track temperature did not appear to affect tyre grip.

Control Tyre

Tyres were open.

Control Additive

Volante Purple.

Case Study Group and Results

Five drivers, running six cars, contributed to this case study across both 13.5 Stock and Modified classes. Unless otherwise stated, comments apply to both classes.

Tyres

One set of tyres was sufficient for the meeting including: 3 practice runs, 6 qualifiers and 3 finals.

We ran one car with untrued tyres. Fronts began the meeting with a diameter of 45.1mm and rears were 46.3mm. Total tyre wear on both front and rear was a reduction of 0.9mm tyre diameter on each tyre for the entire meeting.

The other cars tyres were trued down to: fronts 42mm diameter and rears 43mm diameter (unless otherwise stated). This resulted in a more stable feeling car.

Because tyres were open several different types of tyre were used:

- Ulti XM front, Ulti XS rear – provided good grip and steering.
- Ulti JM front, Ulti GS rear – also provided good grip and steering. These two drivers changed to Ulti XM fronts for qualifying and found the car too twitchy and occasionally traction rolled. Reverting to JM fronts solved this problem.
- Ulti GM front and rear – trued to 39mm front and 40mm rear.

Tyre Preparation

a. Cleaned tyres with a small amount of tyre additive on a rag to remove bits of carpet and debris from the surface of the tyre. Using additive rather than brake cleaner assists to not dry the foam out and keeps it closer to the original compound. If you decide to use brake cleaner, wait 5 minutes for it to evaporate before applying additive.

b. 20 minutes before the run, tyre additive was applied and left to air dry for 15 minutes.

c. 5 minutes before the run, tyres were dried off completely with a cloth. This gave good grip from the first corner onward for the entire 8-minute run. (Experiments putting the car on the track with wet tyres or drying the tyres with a cloth to remove excess additive just before the race, both resulted in a car that would spin out at the first corner and was like driving on ice for the first half of the warm-up lap. After half a lap the tyres generated excellent grip for the 8-minute race.)

d. No tyre warmers were used.

e. All drivers applied additive liberally to the rear tyres.

f. Two drivers did not apply additive to their front tyres as they had sufficient steering.

g. Two drivers applied additive to the inner half of the fronts for the start of the day and reduced it to the inner quarter as the grip came up.

One driver applied additive 35 minutes prior to the race. Full rear and inside quarter on the front. Put the car on the track with wet tyres. Car was taily for the first few corners, but he found that wiping the additive off reduced grip towards the end of the race (an issue not experienced by the other drivers).

The Race Meeting

We arrived on Friday afternoon after a 7-hour drive from Melbourne and went straight into practice.

Car 1: Roche Chassis – 2nd in Stock

The aluminium chassis and rear pod were used.

The first change made was to narrow the rear track width by 2mm to 172mm to generate more bite. This track was tight and brake heavy, so a narrower setting made the car faster in and out of corners.

Reactive caster was increased from 5 to 10 degrees for more initial steering.

The short wheelbase was used for a lighter feeling front end which was not so aggressive (wheelbase was shortened at the front of the car).

The shims were reduced under the rear of the shock from 2mm to 1mm, decreasing the shock angle for more progressive traction (smoother rotation instead of high bite in every corner. Higher bite made the car too "on the edge" to drive quickly).

Harder shock spring was installed to provide more rotation under brakes and slow corners which helped over the infield bumps on this track.

Ran slight cone-in on front tyres for more front bite (approximately 1mm larger diameter on the outside of the tyre than the inside).

Ride height was 3.6mm front and middle, 3.8mm rear.

Changed from 15k to 10k shock oil in side tubes for more roll and the feeling of an aggressive car with plenty of bite, which this driver prefers.

Increased Ackermann by adding a 2mm shim resulting in greater initial steering.

Bodies:
- Protoform AMR was very planted but also too safe and not as fast as the car could be.
- Montech M16 rotated better through tight corners and was therefore faster for this driver's style.

Left to right: CRC (3rd in Modified), Berzerk'd Team Saxo, CRC

Cars 2–4: Team Saxo Chassis and 2 x CRC Chassis – 3rd in Modified

Before arriving, the following changes were made from this teams' typical outdoor asphalt setup:

- Front camber gain was decreased by raising the inside of the upper arm, 3mm in this case.
- A front brace was fitted between the front uprights to reduce flex/grip.
- Ride height was reduced from 5.0mm to around 4.0mm. Due to the bumpy nature at this event, we kept it a little higher than the minimum of 3.0mm.

Gearing was also reduced due to the smaller/tighter track:

- Pinion with one less tooth in Modified.
- Pinion with five fewer teeth in Stock.

During Friday practice it was noted that the car stalled mid-corner, this seemed to be the inner rear wheel lifting. The solution was to widen the rear track width from approximately 169mm to the maximum of 172mm. 169mm works well for a lower grip level on asphalt, but provided too much grip on this carpet track when the optimum grip level had been reached.

During racing it was noted that the cars were getting harder to drive, i.e: too much steering and overly sensitive to input. Two things were changed: the side damper oil was increased from 10k to 20k, and the side spring was softened from 0.5mm to 0.45mm (to make the front tyre work harder by increasing the weight transfer to the outer front tyre rather than a harder spring transferring it to the outer rear).

Bodies:
- Protoform BMR12.1 lacked steering.
- Protoform AMR was better.
- Montech M12 was the preferred body for its aggressive initial turn-in on this particular track. This made a big difference to the "feel" of the car.

Diff tightness was also increased. This gave the car better acceleration off the corners and made it more predictable under braking. This one little change reduced lap-times. With the tighter diff it also required less rebuilding; none of the diffs on these three cars were rebuilt during the weekend.

Car 5: Xray Chassis

First practice was still using asphalt setup with ride height of: 5mm front and 5.5mm rear. Car was traction rolling. Lowering ride height to 4.5mm front and rear resolved the traction rolling. Ride height was further lowered later, but the car stopped traction rolling at 4.5mm ride height.

Car 6: Xray Chassis

- Protoform Strakka body.
- On the first run, ride height was: front 4.4mm, middle 4.8mm, rear 5.2mm. This was reduced to front 3.6mm, middle 4.2mm, rear 4.2mm and the car felt more stable.
- Reduced rear pod droop from 1.5mm to 0.5mm. Car felt more stable.
- Increased the centre damper angle by removing 0.5mm of spacers from under the front of the shock mount. Car had more rear grip.
- The car felt more planted and quicker through the chicane after the changes.
- Other settings remained as the manufacturer's carpet kit setup.
- The car showed good speed so I stayed with 90mm rollout throughout the meeting, although in hindsight a smaller rollout would probably have reduced lap-times.
- After each run, camber was checked and adjusted to prevent tyre coning. The front left tyre showed a small amount of additional wear compared to the front right so was swapped every couple of runs to even out the wear.

- Tyre wear was negligible and ride height was adjusted as necessary to maintain front 3.6mm, middle 4.2mm, and rear 4.2mm throughout the meeting.
- After the second qualifier, the car had sufficient grip to allow harder braking and increased brake force on the ESC from 75% to 100%, and initial brake from 0% to 20%. Drag brake remained at 0%. My fastest lap time dropped by 0.5 seconds.
- Car felt very good and could push as hard as my driving skill allowed for the entire lap.

F1

Case Study Track

Asian On-road Championship, Dandenong, Australia. CRC Carpet. Track temperature was 11–17°C for the entire meeting (52–63°F). Low-Medium grip. Flowing / Mixed track.

Control Tyre

Sweep F1FV5S-HPG front, F1RV53-28RPG rear (Rubber).

Control Additive

Sweep Carpet Grabber X4 #SW0027.

Tyre Preparation

I had a fair idea of the tyre preparation which would work based on last year's event. However, as an experiment, I tried my outdoor asphalt tyre preparation (one application of additive on the rear tyres only and tyre warmers used for 15 minutes on 55°C (131°F)) and the car was barely driveable. Using the tyre preparation in the table below resolved this problem.

Views of tyre preparation carried some common threads as shown in this table:

	Car 1 (TQ/1st) Jan Ratheisky	Car 2 (4th)	Car 3 (5th)	Car 4
Clean Tyres with Brake Cleaner	Y (although would have used additive if allowed by event rules)	Y	Y	Y
Tyre Warmers	Y	Y	N	N
Additive Rear	Full	Full	Full	Full
Additive Process	Multiple applications as needed for track conditions. Last coat 30 min before race.	• Full rear and front inner ¾ and air dry. • Re-apply full rear and front inner ¼ and warm at 58°C rear and 52°C front. • Remove tyre warmers 10 min before race.	• Applied two coats of additive on rear tyres 15 mins apart.	• Apply 40min before race (full rear/ none front), and air dry. Repeat after 20 min. • Just before race apply to rear and front and put the car on the track with wet tyres.
Additive Front	Multiple applications as needed for track conditions. Full width Last coat 20 min before race.	As above.	Inner ½. Increased to slightly more than ½ later in the meeting.	Track temp: 11°C Full 17°C Inner ½

Applying additive twice to the rears was key to obtaining sufficient traction on this cold, medium grip track. No driver wiped their tyres before placing the car on the track.

The Race Meeting

Car 1: Xray X1 2019 – TQ & 1st – Jan Ratheisky

The track was quite slippery compared to European tracks and required many changes from the kit setup:

- Removed anti-roll bar.
- Reduced caster from 9° to 6°.
- Increased rear droop from 1mm to 1.5mm. This provided more rear rotation; the new rear wing mount system makes this possible.
- Increased front droop from 0.5mm to 0.8mm. More on-power rear traction.
- Increased side spring stiffness from c=0.9 to 1.2 and increased side damping oil from 10K to 30K. More stable rear during weight transfer.
- Toe-out from 1.5° to 2°. This gave significantly less initial steering but a more stable car.
- Wider rear from 1mm/side to 2.5mm/side. More rear traction up to the limit of 190mm width.

The following changes were made to fine-tune steering:

- Changed centre shock:
  - Oil from 600cSt to 1000cSt and spring from C2.3 to C2.3-2.6. More mid-corner steering. On-power the traction was ok.
  - Piston holes diameter from 1.1mm to 1.2mm to allow the thicker oil to flow.
- Reduced camber from -2° to -1.5°. More balanced steering. No bite on the track means less camber needed.

Other changes:

- Higher rear wing position from 2 to 1. More high-speed rear traction especially on brake at the end of the straight.
- Wider front width from 0.5mm/side to 1mm/side. This was needed with the control tires to make the bearings fit correctly.

Final Setup Summary:

- Ride height: front 4.2mm, middle 4.4mm, rear 4.6mm.
- Droop: rear 1.5mm, front 0.8mm.
- Shock oil 1000cSt, 25% rebound, 4 hole piston (1.2mm holes), no foam insert, c=2.3-2.6 spring, short shock position.

- Ball Diff setting: medium.
- Side Damper: 30K oil.
- Side springs: black (c=1.2).
- Front springs: kit spring (c=2.0).
- Front kingpin lube: 10k.
- Front Toe-out: 2°.
- Anti-roll bar: none.
- Chassis: hard graphite (experimental chassis, normal graphite would have been better).
- Battery position: cross chassis.
- Front Spoiler: low downforce.
- FDR: 2.41.

Car 2: Yokomo Chassis – 4th

- Ride height: front 4.2mm, 4.4mm middle, 4.6mm rear.
- Rear pod droop 0.6mm.
- -1.5° camber.
- Yokomo hard graphite chassis (Yokomo states: the increased rigidity provides improved steering response and high-speed stability).
- Increased front width.
- This driver runs a 1/12th steering bell crank as he prefers the feel of the steering when using it.
- Car lacked rear-end grip. This was also reported by a lot of other drivers on this surface. Increased the side damper oil to 60K and widened the rear axle width to increase traction. This worked well.
- Further increased side damper oil to 100K and this provided sufficient rear traction.
- Used 10K oil on front kingpins and changed to soft front springs to increase initial steering.

- Changed to ultra-soft side springs to provide more traction.
- Tightened ball diff a little more than normal for increased drive out of corners.
- Increased wheelbase by changing from trailing axles on the steering arms to leading axles. This assisted with initial steering and reduced understeer.

Car 3: Xray Chassis – 5th

Starting Setup:
- Ride height: 4.0mm front, 4.5mm rear.
- Shock oil: 350cSt.
- Spring: Progressive-Soft (Xray part #308263).
- Shock: Long, front mount position.
- Damper tubes: 20K oil.
- Side springs: gold.
- Gear Diff: 1K oil.
- Ackermann: middle position using aluminium adjustable servo saver set (option part #372541).
- Caster: 1 dot at back.
- Camber: 1 dot inwards.
- Front width: 190mm (wide position).
- Rear width: 190mm.
- Rear pod droop: 1mm.
- Front droop: 1mm.
- Anti-roll bar: Soft (1.1mm).
- Gearing 39t pinion and 80t spur (2.05 FDR).
- Chassis has 3 front wheelbase settings; short, middle, and long. Started with middle setting.

Practice Tuning:
- For the initial runs the car was loose and unstable at rear. It was "no good at all."
- Changed to:
    - Short wheelbase at front.
    - Narrow front end.
- This improved stability but it was "still not very good".
- Further changes:
    - Stopped using tyre warmers.
    - Applied two coats of additive on rear tyres ~15 mins apart, inner half width on fronts.

- "This was significantly better, by far! The warmers were definitely not working with these tyres/conditions. Car was now stable and just about had enough rear grip, but now had big understeer."

Race Tuning:
- Changed to a rear wing with slightly more area. This made minimal difference but wasn't worse.
- Changed to minimum Ackermann. Again, this made a small difference, and the car was a bit more predictable. "Overall though it was still not rotating through corners enough and significant understeer remained."
- "I chatted with Jan Ratheisky and asked what I should do to get more rotation in the corners, but still have the rear grip it needs, he suggested the following:
    - Replace the gear diff with the ball diff.
    - Wider rear axles spacers +2mm.
    - Change shock from long to short mounting position."
- These changes made a positive improvement. The car had much better rotation through the constant radius apexes.
- I then increased the width of the front tyre additive slightly in the remaining races, to slightly increase the steering.

Car 4: Xray Chassis

- Ride height: front 4.4mm, 4.6mm middle, 4.8mm rear.
- Rear pod droop 0.5mm.
- -1.5° camber.
- Removed 1mm shim from under the front shock mount. The increased shock angle providing more rear grip at the expense of on-power steering.
- Soft side springs for greater traction.
- 5K oil on front kingpins.
- Soft front spings for more initial steering.
- Car was too lively when accelerating out of the corners which occasionally caused oversteer. Added -100% throttle expo on radio. This was too slow. Changed to -70% which solved the oversteer while allowing aggressive use of the trigger. Improved lap consistency and my fastest lap.
- When track was cold (11°C) the car lacked braking, turned up brake EPA to 100% on radio. When track warmed up (17°C) changed brake EPA back to 80% (which is where this driver normally runs it).
- The car was hooked up and drove well.

Overall Comment

It is interesting to note the difference in setup between the various cars. In particular, the world champion's setup for car 1, and the club racer's setup for car 4. Both were running Xray X1 chassis, although car 4 was several years older.

The driver of car 4 was happy with their setup, for their skill level; the car was easy to drive, and he finished in the middle of the field. That's not to say further setup changes wouldn't have made the car easier for this driver to drive it more quickly.

This was a challenging low grip carpet track on which to setup a fast car. Jan Ratheisky quickly identified the many setup changes required, giving him a significant advantage.

Asphalt Case Studies

Starting Setup

If you have not raced at a particular track before, we recommend starting with your chassis manufacturer's base asphalt setup. You may also wish to search your chassis manufacturer's website for another driver's setup at that track so that you can note changes they made. We do not recommend using another driver's setup without knowing why they made the changes they did. However, it can be very useful to note the differences to the manufacturer's base asphalt setup and then try each change, one at a time, and note whether it feels better or worse.

Changes Compared to Carpet

1. Asphalt tracks tend to be bumpier than carpet and therefore you should use a higher ride height.
2. Asphalt generally provides less grip than a carpet track. Therefore, the car will normally be less stiff in order to provide sufficient grip.
3. Tyre wear on asphalt is significantly greater than on carpet.
4. Asphalt tracks are normally outdoors and therefore track temperatures will change throughout the day.

Case Study Track

Pan Car Challenge, TFTR Track, Melbourne, Australia. Medium grip asphalt (bumpy in places). Fast, flowing track. One day event.

Track Temperature

Track temperature varied. Practice was 35°C (95°F) in the early morning but cooled slightly during the day, varying during racing from 28–32°C (82–90°F). The grip came up during the day as rubber and additive was laid down. The small variation in track temperature from first practice to the last final did not impact tyre choice in F1, where tyres were open.

Control Tyre

1/12th – Control tyres: Ulti JM Front, Ulti XSS Rears. Two sets per entry.
F1 – Tyres were open.

Control Additive

Additive was open.

1/12th

Case Study Group and Results

Three drivers contributed to this case study across both 13.5 Stock and Modified classes. Unless otherwise stated, comments apply to both Stock and Modified.

Tyres

One set of tyres was sufficient in Stock. Two sets were used in Modified. Meeting format was open practice, 3 qualifiers and 3 finals. All cars ran with untrued tyres.

Stock Tyres

Fronts began the meeting with a diameter of 45.1mm and rears were 46.3mm. Total tyre wear on both front and rear in Stock was a reduction of approximately 2.7mm tyre diameter on each tyre for the entire meeting.

Modified Tyres

The winner of the Modified class provided these insights. Normally, he always trues new tyres to about 42.5mm rears for asphalt, with the fronts approximately 0.5mm smaller. However, at this event, we only had 2 sets to last 6 races and they were an extremely soft foam compound. Therefore, run-time was a concern and for that reason he left the tyres untrued. Something he described as, "a very weird experience for me!"

1. New Ultis were: Rear 46.5mm, Front 45.5mm.
2. After first run: Rear L45.0mm/R45.5mm.
3. After second run: Rear L44.2mm/R43.8mm, Front L43.7mm/R43.7mm.
4. After third run: Rear L42.8mm/R42.8mm, Front L42.4mm/R43.0mm.
5. Rotation left to right after each run was essential to always start with the larger on the left side for this predominantly right-hand track. Normally, this driver would re-true them equal after each run, but didn't this time to maximise the diameter given the 2 set tyre limit.
6. The second new set, again untrued, were used for the finals. Although the first set had sufficient foam for one more run, I chose to repeat the three-run cycle used in qualifiers for the finals.

Xray X12 '19 (1st in Modified)

Because additive was open, several different types were used and these are noted below under each car.

Tyre Preparation

Views of tyre preparation varied between drivers as shown in this table:

	Car 1 (1st Mod)	Car 2 (1st Stock)	Car 3
Clean Tyres with Brake Cleaner	Y [1]	N [3]	Y
Tyre Warmers	50C [2]	N	N
Additive Rear	Full	Full	Full
Additive Front	Full	Inner ¾	None
Additive Process	[2]	Air dry for 35 min	Air dry for 15 min
Wiping Process	Wipe fully 5 min before run	None [4]	[5]

1. "I used brake cleaner to clean the tyres. My testing over many years showed no negative effects. However, I find the brake cleaner enables the cleaner foam/rubber to accept the additive far better. Wait 5 minutes for brake cleaner to evaporate before applying additive. I clean the tyres as soon as possible after marshalling, measure diameters, rotate and then apply the additive so it has maximum time to soak in before the next run."

2. "I use tyre warmers (50°C), not to have hot tyres on the grid, but predominantly to help the tyre better accept the additive. The heat relaxes the 'up-tight' tyre polymers making more space for the additive to melt and 'nestle in'. Remove the tyre warmers approximately 10 minutes before the run (no wiping yet though). Wipe thoroughly approximately 5 minutes before the run."

3. Cleaned tyres with a small amount of tyre additive on a rag to remove dust and debris from the surface of the tyre. Using additive rather than brake cleaner, assists not to dry the foam out and keeps it closer to the original compound (in this drivers opinion).

4. "Put the car on the track with wet tyres. Car oversteered for the first few corners but I found that wiping the additive off reduced grip towards the end of the race." This issue was not experienced by the other drivers.

5. Dried tyres with a cloth to remove excess additive just before the race. This resulted in a car that would spin out at the first corner and was like driving on ice for the first half of the warm-up lap. After half a lap the tyres generated excellent grip for the 8-minute race.

The Race Meeting

Car 1: Xray Chassis – 1st in Modified

Xray does not have a recommended kit asphalt setup. The following setup was used from the last club meeting at this track:

Starting setup:

1. Ride Height: Rear 4.8mm, Front: 4.3mm (usually aim for front being 0.5mm lower than rear).
2. Pod droop: 0.8mm.
3. Width: Rear 170mm & Front +1mm concentric (i.e: wider than standard setting. This reduces front end steering to make the car easier to drive, at the expense of slightly slower lap times).
4. Battery: cross chassis, full rearward.
5. Camber: -1° each side (note: after each run adjust as needed to react to tyre coning).
6. Caster: 11° up from the kit setting of 5.5° by increasing the reactive caster to make the car react quicker and provide more steering.
7. Front toe-out: 0.5mm each side.
8. Kingpins: Tamiya anti-wear grease for damping, kit Gold C3.5 spring.
9. Main shock: long extension, forward position, 450cSt oil, kit Gold C1.8 spring.
10. Side links: outer position, no shims.
11. Side damping: used optional shock damper with 600cSt oil.

Changes made:

1. After Practice 1 changed from a ball differential to a gear diff (the first time this driver had tried one). "The gear diff was awesome with a lot of rotation and allowed me to really rotate and drive the car out of the corner (700 cSt oil). It provided a much more reactive feel to driving the car, needing an even smoother application of steering and throttle inputs on this asphalt medium/low grip. But I liked it a lot!"
2. No changes were made after Practice 2. Re-lubed the kingpins ready for the first qualifier.
3. During Qualifier 1 the car understeered. It also had decent rear stability and could therefore handle more front bite. Changed the front track width back to the standard 'middle' concentric setting i.e: from wider setting back to narrower 'standard' setting.

4. During Qualifier 2 this added more steering mainly mid-corner and slightly on exit. Car still had a little understeer. Therefore, changed the main shock spring. "I had just received the progressive Xray springs, so was keen to try these for the first time." Changed to progressive C1.4~1.9.
5. During Qualifier 3 this "made a great improvement to increase steering on corner entry and a decent amount of mid-corner too. Marginal difference on exit phase. The car was good, but could still use more rotation and steering, especially mid-corner and exit if the rear still sticks under throttle. I therefore changed the rear wheelbase to the shorter option (~1mm shorter). I also just received the rear concentric axle bearing holders and tried those."
6. During Final 1 "this was an excellent improvement to overall lateral rotation through all 3 phases of the corner, especially for high-speed corners on throttle. I was happy with the car. I would have liked to try swapping back to the side damper tubes (instead of side shock) which would allow battery forward positioning options, but ran out of time between runs. I cleaned and re-lubed the steering kingpins with 50K silicone oil instead of the Tamiya grease."
7. During Final 2 "I couldn't detect any difference from the type of lube used, although it probably benefitted from a good clean to remove the grit. I didn't change anything for the last final, just the usual tyre prep and ride-heights adjustment to compensate for the tyre wear (did this after every run of course)."

Additive:
"Additive is where science meets art. I used mostly FX with 12.5% tyre tweak and 16% buggy grip."

Body:
- Protoform AMR-12 lightweight: It had very good stability and consistency as well as looking great.
- Protoform BMR-12: gave car immense understeer.
- Protoform Strakka: while it delivered fast individual lap times, was generally less stable and susceptible to unpredictable on-power oversteer. It was therefore not fast over race distance.

Car 2: Roche Chassis – 1st in Stock

This driver used the same setup as they used on carpet at the RCRA Australian Indoor On-road Championships on page *111* (car 1), except for the following changes:

- Carbon chassis and rear pod were used.
- 4.5mm ride height.
- 1.2mm rear pod droop.
- LG2 additive.
- Body: The Protoform AMR was used. Compared to the Montech M16, the AMR generated a little more grip on this track.
- Although the driver felt "there was additional pace available in the car, it was fast and felt great, so no further setup changes were made after the qualifiers."

Car 3: Xray Chassis

Xray do not have a recommended kit asphalt setup. The following changes were made to the kit carpet setup:

- Ride height: 5mm front, 5.2mm middle, 5.4mm rear.
- Rear pod droop 1.5mm.
- Total width: front 165mm, rear 170mm.
- Battery position: cross chassis.
- Camber: -1°
- 3000cSt lube on front kingpins.
- Side Damper lube 10,000cSt.
- Additive: Volante Purple
- Body: Protoform Strakka.
- Reduced brake force on the ESC from to 100% to 75%, and initial brake from 20% to 0%. Drag brake remained at 0%.
- The car showed good speed with a 90mm rollout throughout the meeting.
- After each run, camber was re-checked and adjusted to prevent coning. The front left tyre showed a small amount of additional wear compared to the front right, so these were swapped every couple of runs to even out the wear.
- "Car felt very good and I could push as hard as my driving skill allowed for the entire lap."

F1

The Race Meeting

Car 1: Xray Chassis – TQ

Tyre

Tyres were open. Given the track temperature, I would normally use Ride GR but decided on a tyre I hadn't raced with yet, but which performed very well in practice. Volante Green front, Double Pink rear (Rubber). These performed very well all meeting and only one set was used.

Additive

"Buggy Grip and Trinity Tyre Tweak. There may be better additive on the market now but years ago I settled on this two-step preparation for rubber tyres which has served me well, as follows."

Tyre Preparation

1. Cleaned tyres with brake cleaner to remove dust and debris from the surface of the tyre. Wait a few minutes for it to evaporate before applying additive.
2. At least 20 minutes before the run Buggy Grip tyre additive was applied and left to air dry for 5 minutes (assumes a warm day).
3. At least 15 minutes before the run Trinity Tyre Tweak was applied.
4. Tyre warmers set to 60°C (140°F) were applied for at least 15 minutes.
5. If any area of the tyres remained wet from additive then they were gently wiped off.
6. This gave good grip from the first corner onward for the entire 5-minute run.
7. Additive was applied liberally to:
    a. The rear tyres.
    b. To the inner ½ of the front tyres.

Setup

Xray does not have a recommended kit asphalt setup. The following changes were made to the kit carpet setup:

- Shims under front of shock reduced to 0mm (i.e: shims removed).

- Ride height: 5mm front, 5.2mm middle, 5.4mm rear.
- Rear pod droop 1.5mm.
- Softened the front springs (from kit springs to one spring rate softer) to increase steering.
- 35wt main shock and side shock fluid.
- -1.5° camber.
- Battery position: inline.
- Ackermann position 1 (at front of steering arm) to increase cornering speed on this fast flowing track.
- Toe out: 2°.
- Diff setting: tighten and then back off ¼ turn.
- Final Drive Ratio: 2.57 with Trinity Monster Max 21.5.

Car 2: Xray Chassis – 1st

Starting Setup

Kit settings and parts plus the following:
- Ride height: 4.3mm front, 4.8mm rear.
- Shock oil: 350cSt (down from the kit 600cSt) for faster weight transfer to the front-end for initial turn-in and also to the rear-end for on exit power.
- Spring: Progressive-Soft (Xray part #308263).
- Shock: Long, front mount position.
- Damper tubes: 20K.
- Side springs: gold.
- Gear Diff: 1K oil (Xray recommend 500–1K for low traction conditions, and 2K–5K for medium-high traction. "I deemed the TFTR track condition as low to medium and chose 1K").
- Ackermann: middle position using aluminium adjustable servo saver set (option part #372541).
- Caster: 6deg (1 dot forward).
- Camber: 1deg (1 dot in).
- Front width: 190mm (wide position).
- Rear width: 190mm.
- Rear pod droop: 1mm.
- Front droop: 1mm.
- Anti-roll bar: Soft (1.1mm).
- Gearing 40t pinion and 80t spur (FDR 2.0).

Case Studies

Practice Tuning

- I tried various tyres in practice including:
    - Rear: Ride S1 soft – not good, minimal grip.
    - Rear: Pit Shimizu PS-575: massive oversteer on this hot track.
    - Rear: Ride R1 – selected for racing.
    - Front tyre PS-573: lots of push (useful if needed in future).
    - Front tyre PS-571: good balance but became very hot after a few laps causing oversteer.
    - Front tyre PS-574: "Pushes a little, a nice feel."
    - Front tyre Volante #VF1-FMS: "Quite good! Bit of understeer – nice to drive. Selected for racing."
- Side spring: Silver was slightly more stable.
- Main spring: Hard progressive (Xray part #308264) more reactive on turn-in.
- Tight screw centre top plate: very stable (Screw connecting the "graphite plate for mounts (#371096)" to the "top deck (#376232)" with 3x6x3mm spacer. You can run without screw/spacer completely OR with loose screw and hard or soft spacer OR tight screw with spacer).

Race Notes

- Traction Additive: Full rear and 25%, or slightly less, on front, inner edge of tyres. Used Buggy Grip as this always works and evaporates well/quickly. Good for the warm to hot conditions as it doesn't seem to overheat the tyres as much as some additives can.
- Re-lube side damper sparingly: 100K. "This would have been too heavy for my 1/12th scale but worked well for my heavier F1 car."
- Back to softer progressive centre spring. This made the car a little calmer and not as aggressive into the corner.
- Back to kit Gold side springs. Silver spring was causing aggressive/twitchy behaviour.
- 0.5mm less front droop (now 0.5mm total) – fractionally slower best lap time but car easier to drive and more consistent overall.
- Volante fronts were very stable, but slightly too much push. Removed front sway bar to get slightly more steering.
- Switched to Pit Shimizu PS-571 front tyre but too much steering, rear breaking away.
- Switched to Pit Shimizu PS-574 front tyre which provided a lot of steering but no oversteer. Faster although a little harder to drive. Kept using these.

- Overall the Ride R1 provided the best rear grip [Author's note: Ride has replaced the Ride R1 with the Ride GR tyre]. The front was a challenge to get right. After trying various combinations noted above, I preferred the Pit Shimizu PS-574 as it provided good steering with a little bit of push, but never over gripped against the rear. The car had a little push as a result which is not as quick as a car with no push. However, the stability was worth it and would allow fine-tuning to increase the front grip given more testing time.

Car 3: Yokomo Chassis – 2nd

- Ride height: front 4.2mm, 4.4mm middle, 4.6mm rear.
- Toe-out 1.5°.
- Silver (medium) front kingpin springs.
- -1.5° camber.
- Caster 9°.
- Kingpin spacers: 3mm above arm and 0mm below. 0.2mm below spring.
- Shock shims: 2mm under front and 2mm under rear.
- Motor cooling fan fitted.
- Side springs silver.
- Side dampers: started with 30k lube. Reduced to 20k to fine-tune steering.
- Battery installed across the chassis.
- Increased front width.
- I run a 1/12th steering bell crank as I prefer the feel of the steering when using it. Ackermann is significantly less than kit.
- Ride GR tyres.
- Tyre warmers at 60°C.
- LG2 additive: full width of rear tyres, inner 1/3 of fronts.
- FDR 2.28:1.

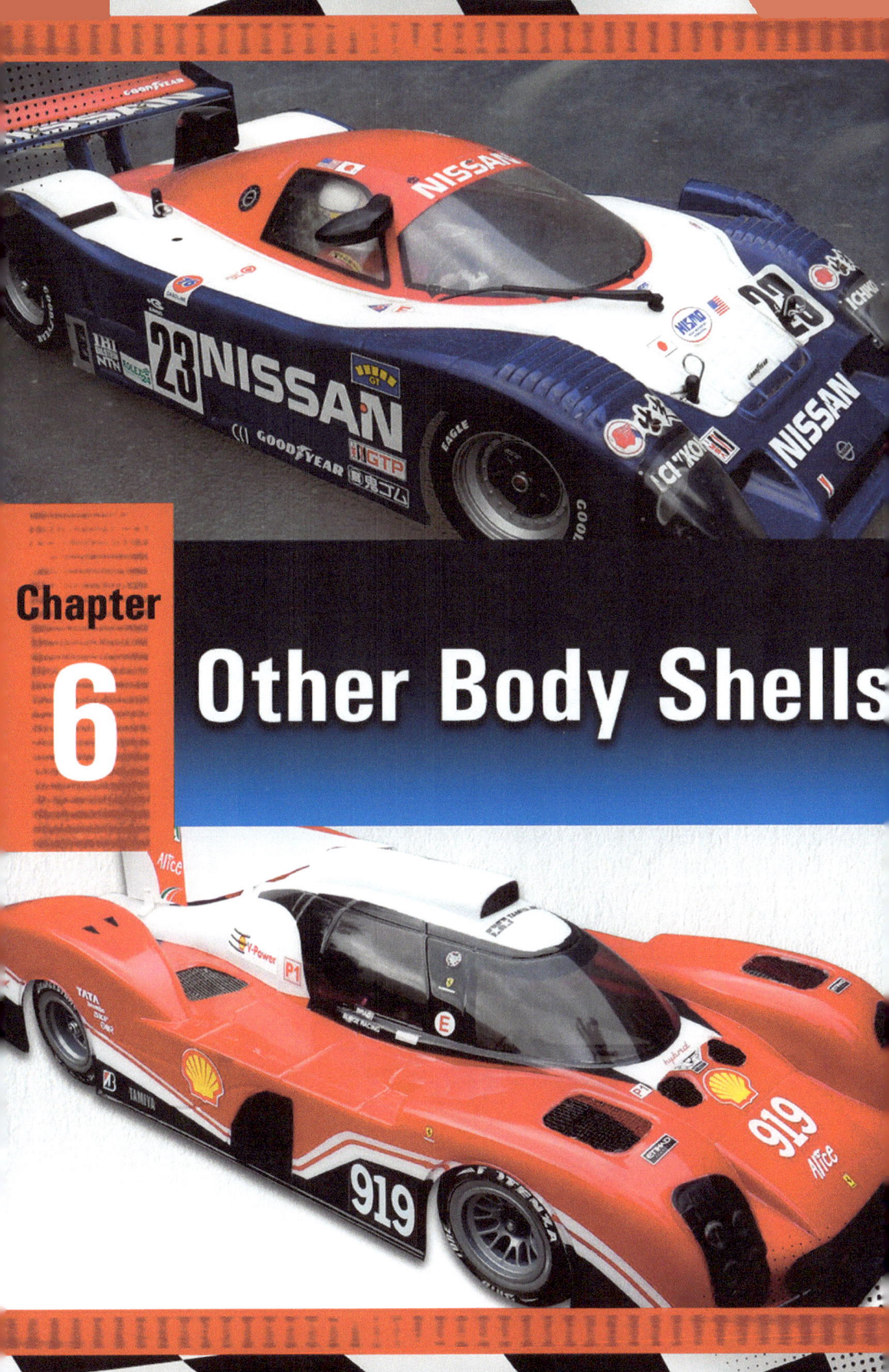

Chapter 6
Other Body Shells

GT12

The GT12 class are 1/12th cars with GT body shells. Group C shells are sometimes allowed (check your local rules):

LMP1

LMP1 shells are available for 1/12th and F1. The following photos are F1 cars. The front end is modified using a third-party kit to provide support for two body posts:

Group C

Group C shells are available for 1/12th and F1. The following photos are 1/12th:

Alonso & Webber Model

When Fernando Alonso gave Mark Webber a ride back to the pits at the Singapore Grand Prix in 2013, S37 Racing created this fantastic tribute.

Alonso's F138 Scuderia Ferrari (2013) was modelled using a Tamiya F2012 body shell mounted on a Tamiya F104 car. The coanda exhaust cowl and front nose were scratch-built, and the suspension was modified to four-wheel independent. The steering wheel, driver's arms and head all turn with the steering servo.

Awarded the prize for Scale Colour at the Tamiya Plamodel Factory Shinbashi RC Modelers contest (2014).

Appendix A – Glossary

This section explains the common terms used in this book, where they are not otherwise explained as part of the relevant chapter.

For a diagram of car parts refer to page 40.

Chunking

Foam tyres may lose a chunk of foam, often on the outside of the rim. This is called chunking. Causes include: a crash, car-to-car contact, or if a tyre is no longer correctly glued to the rim (as the edge of the tyre may lift during cornering).

Corner Entry

Corner entry is when you first turn-in to a corner until you stop turning the steering wheel on your radio. The car begins to roll. This sets up the line to be taken through the corner. It is often defined as the segment of the turn from the turn-in point to the apex.

Corner Exit

Corner exit is where you are reducing the steering input and commence accelerating. The car starts to roll back level. It is often defined as the segment of the turn from the apex until the corner has been completed.

ESC

The Electronic Speed Controller (ESC) controls the speed and direction of the motor.

Mid-corner

Mid-corner is the part of the corner where steering input is constant (the steering wheel is turned at a constant angle and is neither increasing nor decreasing). The car is at maximum roll. The apex is normally taken during the mid-corner (refer to page 24).

Off-power Steering

This is when trying to change the direction of the car while the throttle is neutral or under braking. Letting off the power causes the car to dive at the front and rise at the rear. Braking causes this effect to increase i.e: the car dives more at the front under braking.

On-power Steering

This is when trying to change the direction of the car while holding or increasing the throttle. For example, coming out of a slow corner and then accelerating through a sweeper, the driver is accelerating while changing the steering angle. Under power, the car will rise at the front and squat at the rear.

Oversteer (Loose)

Oversteer is a cornering situation where the rear wheels do not track behind the front wheels but instead slide out toward the outside of the turn. Oversteer can cause the car to spin.

Put simply, when you turn into a corner, oversteer is when the car turns more than you expected. It is often referred to as the car being 'loose' or where the driver 'loses' the back-end.

Rear wheel drive cars are generally more prone to oversteer, in particular when applying power in a tight corner. This occurs because the rear tyres must handle both the lateral cornering force and engine torque.

Sudden weight transfer, such as swerving, can cause oversteer.

For solutions to oversteer refer to the checklist for *Too Much Steering (Oversteer)* on page *148*.

Understeer (Push)

Understeer is a cornering situation where the car turns less sharply than the driver intends. This typically occurs when the front tyres have insufficient traction for the car to follow the intended line.

Put simply, when you turn into a corner, understeer is when the car turns less than you expected. It is also often referred to as 'pushing', or refusing to turn-in.

Too much speed when entering a corner can also cause understeer.

It is common for a manufacturer's base setup to have a slight tendency to understeer by default. If a car understeers slightly, it tends to be more stable (within the realms of a driver of average ability).

For solutions to understeer refer to the checklist for *Not Enough Steering (Understeer)* on page *149*.

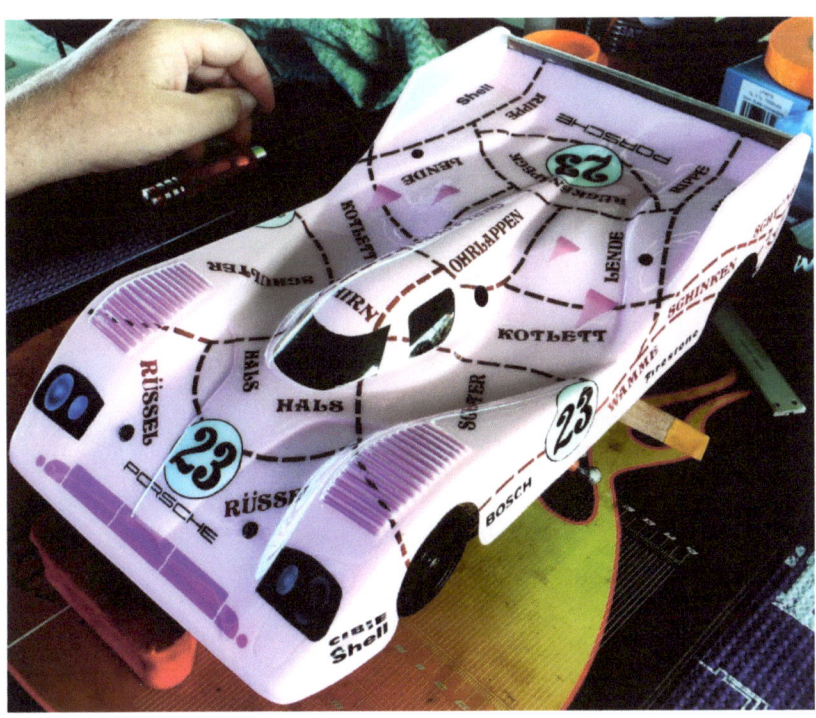

Appendix B – eBook

This book is available as an eBook at a discount to those that have already purchased the physical book.

The eBook is available for any device with a web browser: Windows and Mac, iOS and Android, etc.

Additional eBook features include:

- Full-text search.

- Annotate content, including:
    - Highlight text.
    - Add your own notes to any text.

- Annotations are available across all of your devices, i.e: make notes on your phone and they are available on your tablet and computer.

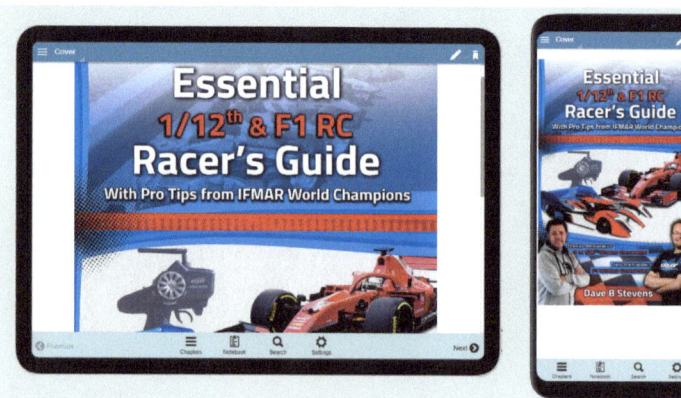

Visit www.DaveBStevens.com for details and to purchase.

Appendix C – Checklists

Quick Reference

After Run Checks	143
Change of Direction (Chicane)	144
Easier to Drive – How To	144
Fast Sweeper Cornering	145
New Car – How to Set Up	145
Re-building a Car	146
Rear Traction – How to Increase	147
Steering	148
Too Much Steering (Oversteer)	148
General Oversteer	148
Oversteer at Corner Entry	148
Oversteer at Mid-corner	148
Oversteer at Corner Exit	149
Oversteer On-power	149
Not Enough Steering (Understeer)	149
General Understeer	149
Understeer at Corner Entry	149
Understeer at Mid-corner	150
Understeer at Corner Exit or at High Speed	150
Steering Response Changes for No Apparent Reason	150
Traction Rolling	151
Troubleshooting	151
Car 'Hops' or 'Chatters' Across the Track	151
Car Wanders on the Straight	151
Tyres Picking Up Carpet Debris from Track	151
Inconsistent Handling	152
Lacking Acceleration or Started Oversteering	152

After Run Checks

After a race or practice run check your car over. The car should have a battery installed:

1. Check tyres:
   a. Are still glued properly to the rim and re-glue if needed. Try and peel the tyre edge back with your thumb and if it comes away from the rim, add some CA glue to fix it back to the rim. This applies for foam and rubber tyres. Foam tyres coming unglued can cause chunking.
   b. Look for cracks on the rim. If cracked, then replace, or CA glue may help for a short period.
   c. If foam tyres:
      i. Check for chunking (chunks of foam missing from the tyre).
      ii. Check for Tyre Coning, i.e: either the inside or outside of the tyre is wearing at a faster rate, causing the tyre to "cone". Check Camber and adjust as necessary to prevent coning (refer page 44).
      iii. Ride Height – The car's ride height decreases as the foam tyres wear down to smaller diameters. Tyres may wear at different rates front-to-back and left-to-right, because the track may have more corners, or corners harder on the tyres, in one direction. This may cause a car with uneven ride height at all four corners. If necessary, swap tyres left to right to maintain even wear. Some racers will true tyres to maintain even ride height. Refer to Ride Height on page 68.
2. Push the front wheels to full lock in both directions and check for binding.
3. Kingpins should move up and down smoothly when the front suspension is compressed. If not, then check the kingpins are smooth (polish if needed), are not bent (replace) and have the correct lubrication (refer to Front Springs & Lube on page 81).
4. Check the rear pod moves freely in all directions, if it doesn't refer to Tweak on page 98.
5. Turn the car over and hold the main chassis in your hand without holding the rear pod. Use a straight edge such as a steel ruler to check:
   a. The main chassis appears flat.
   b. The rear pod and main chassis are flat relative to each other.

If there is an issue with (a) or (b) refer to Tweak on page 98.

6. Put down the straight edge and twist the rear pod slightly one way to simulate cornering. When you let the rear pod go, it should return to being in the same plane as the main chassis. Now twist the other way and let go. If the rear pod does not return to the same plane as the main chassis, in either direction, then refer to Setting Side Spring Preload (Coin Trick) on page *82* (or if you have a T-Bar car then refer to page *86*).
7. Check the tightness of the diff (refer to page *55*).

Some racers will put their car on a setup station after each run and partially disassemble the car to ensure it is operating correctly. This may identify further issues and, while not necessary after every run, it can be a good idea prior to a critical race.

Change of Direction (Chicane)

If the car does not change directions quickly then:

1. Spring (side) – harder. Page *82*.
2. Lower ride height if practical. Page *68*.
3. Less Ackermann. Page *41*.

Easier to Drive – How To

Listed in the recommended order. Make one change at a time and check the result:

1. Ackermann – reduce. Page *40*.
2. Side Links – outer position, i.e: the side link is not angled with both side links parallel to each other. Page *78*.
3. Camber – decrease. Page *44*.
4. Camber Gain – decrease. Page *46*.
5. Caster – decrease. Page *47*.
6. Reactive Caster – decrease. Page *49*.
7. Steering Linkage Angle – increase. Page *83*.
8. Track Width (rear) – wider. Page *90*.
9. Track Width (front) – wider. Page *89*.
10. Side Damper – increase viscosity. Page *50*.
11. Side Damper – flatter angle. Page *50*.
12. Battery Position – cross chassis, move forward. Page *43*.

Fast Sweeper Cornering

To increase corner speed through fast sweepers:

1. Side Damping – higher viscosity oil. Slower chassis roll softens steering in fast sweepers. Page *50*.

New Car – How to Set Up

1. If you haven't built an RC car before, we recommend building it exactly as shown in the instruction manual. However, if you are experienced, we recommend building the car using a setup for your local track. Refer to Setup Sheets on page *20*.
2. When building, ensure that you don't cause your car to be tweaked. Follow the instructions in the chapter on *Tweak* on page *98* to ensure the rear pod moves freely, and screws are tightened in the correct order to prevent artificially twisting the chassis.
3. Before assembling each section of the car, refer to the relevant section of *Car Setup Reference* on page *39* for tips.
4. Place the electronics but don't fix in place yet. Balance the car side to side and then fix the electronics in place (refer to page *94*).
5. Check that the motor wires don't bind on the chassis or the body.
6. Program the ESC (refer to page *60*).
7. Program the radio (refer to page *66*).
8. Set the ride height (refer to page *68*).
9. Set the droop (refer to page *58*).
10. Re-check the ride height as changing the rear droop will change the ride height. If you change the ride height, re-check the rear droop.
11. Set the toe (refer to page *87*).
12. Set the camber (refer to page *44*).
13. Re-check the ride height as changing the camber will change the front ride height. If you change the ride height, re-check the camber.
14. Set side spring preload using the coin trick (refer to page *82*, or if you have a T-Bar car, then refer to page *86*).
15. When you first test the car, keep an eye on motor temperature (refer to page *65*).

Checklists - Appendix

Re-building a Car

If you buy a car second hand or haven't used your car for some time then we recommend:

1. Check the car to ensure it is not tweaked. Follow the instructions in *Tweak* on page *98*.
2. Re-build the centre shock (refer to page *51*).
3. Re-grease the side damper tubes (refer to page *50*) or re-build the side shock if it uses one.
4. Check that the front springs are both the same length and of the same type. Repeat for the side springs.
5. Lubricate the kingpins (refer to page *81*).
6. Check the various shims which control the setup and ensure the same number and thickness of shims are used on both sides of the car (left = right).
7. Check the bearings spin freely.
8. Re-build the differential (refer to page *55*).
9. Ensure there is a small amount of play in the rear axle (side-to-side) to ensure it rotates freely and does not bind.
10. Check the gearing (refer to page *61*).
11. Place the electronics but don't fix in place yet. Balance the car side to side and fix the electronics in place (refer to page *94*).
12. Check that the motor wires don't bind on the chassis or the body.
13. Program the ESC (refer to page *60*).
14. Program the radio (refer to page *66*).
15. Set the ride height (refer to page *68*).
16. Set the droop (refer to page *58*).
17. Re-check the ride height as changing the rear droop will change the ride height. If you change the ride height, re-check the rear droop.
18. Set the toe (refer to page *87*).
19. Set the camber (refer to page *44*).
20. Re-check the ride height as changing the camber will change the front ride height. If you change the ride height, re-check the camber.
21. Set side spring preload using the coin trick (refer to page *82*, or if you have a T-Bar car, then refer to page *86*).
22. When you first test the car, keep an eye on motor temperature (refer to page *65*).

Note that the above does not list every single setting that can be checked, but it is the minimum that we recommend.

Rear Traction – How to Increase

Listed in the recommended order. Make one change at a time and check the result. If the car has insufficient rear traction or is oversteering or spinning out then:

1. Softer Rear Tyre. Page *91*.
2. Side Damping – if your car manufacturer offers the choice of side damping tubes or a side shock, the latter is better for low-medium traction conditions. Page *50*.
3. Side Damping tubes or shock – thicker oil. Page *50*.
4. Ride Height – lower rear ride height compared to the front. Page *68*.
5. Centre Shock – add shims at the rear or reduce shims at the front of the shock mount. Page *54*.
6. Centre Shock – lower viscosity oil, softer spring. Page *51*.
7. Battery Position – forward. Page *43*.
8. T-bar – looser screw. Page *85*.
9. Wing (rear F1) – larger wing or mounted higher or increase the upper wing angle (if adjustable). Page *97*.

If your car has been handling well and then begins to lose rear grip here is a checklist of potential causes:

1. Rubber tyres – Are the tyres cold? – Make sure you do a couple of warm-up laps or use tyre warmers if necessary.
2. Rubber tyres – Track Temperature – has the track temperature changed? Are the tyres you are using the correct ones for the new temperature?
3. All tyres – Tyre gluing – check your tyres to see if any of them have come unglued.
4. Differential – is the differential still set correctly?
5. Rear wing – has the rear wing been damaged?
6. Screws – are all the chassis screws done up properly? Losing screws can cause unpredictable handling.

Checklists - Appendix

Steering

Too Much Steering (Oversteer)

If the car has too much steering, it can be difficult to drive and may cause oversteer.

Listed in the recommended order. Make one change at a time and check the result:

General Oversteer

1. Additive – reduce on front tyres. Page 92.
2. Radio – reduce servo End Point Adjustment (EPA). If the amount of steering is correct, but you'd like to reduce how quickly the car turns into the corner, then reduce the Steering Curve (Expo). Page 66.
3. Spring (front) – harder. Page 81.
4. Damping (side) – higher viscosity oil. Page 50.
5. Spring (side) – softer. Page 82.
6. Steering Linkage Angle – increase. Page 83.
7. Battery Position – cross chassis and forward. Page 43.
8. Camber – decrease. Page 44.
9. Droop (Front) – decrease. Page 60.
10. Ride Height – make the front ride height the same as the rear ride height. Page 68.
11. Roll Centre (rear) – lower. Page 78.
12. Camber Gain – decrease. Page 46.
13. Centre Shock – if location can be changed then move towards the front. Page 55.
14. Wing (front F1) – select a wing with less downforce. Page 97.

Oversteer at Corner Entry

1. Ackermann – decrease. Page 40.
2. Track Width (rear) – wider. Page 88.
3. Track Width (front) – wider. Page 88.

Oversteer at Mid-corner

1. Track Width (rear) – wider. Page 88.
2. Wheel Base – longer. Page 96.

Oversteer at Corner Exit

1. Track Width (rear) – narrower. Narrower rear track width increases rear grip at corner exit. Page *88*.
2. Centre Shock – softer spring to reduce drive of the car coming out of the corner and therefore less likely to spin out at corner exit. Page *53*.

Oversteer On-power

1. Centre Shock – shim higher at rear for less on-power steering. Page *54*.
2. Centre Shock – softer spring to reduce drive of the car coming out of the corner and therefore less likely to spin out at corner exit. Page *53*.

Not Enough Steering (Understeer)

Listed in the recommended order. Make one change at a time and check the result. If the car has insufficient steering:

General Understeer

1. Ride Height – check the front ride height is lower than the rear ride height. Page *68*.
2. Additive – increase on front tyres. Page *92*.
3. Spring (Front) – softer. Page *81*.
4. Side Damping – lower viscosity oil. Page *50*.
5. Battery Position – rearward. Page *43*.
6. Camber – increase. Page *44*.
7. Caster – increase. Car may be harder to drive. Page *47*.
8. Camber Gain – increase. Page *46*.
9. Track Width (front) – narrower. Page *89*.
10. Roll Centre (rear) – raise. Page *78*.
11. Wing (front F1) – select a wing with greater downforce. Page *97*.

Understeer at Corner Entry

1. Reactive Caster – increase. More entry steering, less mid-corner steering. Page *49*.
2. Toe Out – increase. Increases corner entry steering at the cost of mid-corner and exit steering. Page *87*.
3. Ackermann – increase. Page *40*.

Understeer at Mid-corner

1. Toe Out – decrease. Increases mid-corner and exit steering at the cost of corner entry steering. Page 87.
2. Reactive Caster – decrease. Decreasing will provide more mid-corner steering at the cost of corner entry steering. Page 49.
3. Side Links – if your car has the option, then use the innermost hole to angle the front of the side link towards the centre of the car, providing more mid-corner steering. Page 78.
4. Wheel Base – shorter provides more mid-corner steering. Page 96.

Understeer at Corner Exit or at High Speed

1. Toe Out – decrease. Increases exit and mid-corner steering at the cost of corner entry steering. Page 87.
2. Centre Shock – shim flatter (less shock angle) for more on-power steering. Page 54.
3. Centre Shock – harder spring for more on-power steering. Page 53.
4. Droop (Front) – increase. Page 60.
5. Droop (Rear) – increase. Page 58.

Steering Response Changes for No Apparent Reason

If the car was steering correctly and no longer is, then:

1. Are the front top steering arms bent?
2. Is the bottom steering arm sitting parallel with the chassis, or has it shifted?
3. Do the front arms move up and down on the springs and return to rest correctly?
4. Has the servo horn stripped?
5. Is the servo working correctly?
6. Is the car tweaked? (Refer to page 98).

Traction Rolling

Traction rolling is when the car is cornering, and it rolls over. It often occurs because the chassis has reached the limit of the amount it can roll but needs to roll more. Because the chassis cannot roll any further, the car rolls over.

Listed in the recommended order. Make one change at a time and check the result. To reduce or eliminate traction rolling:

1. Front Wing (F1 only) – Check that your front wing does not touch the ground during cornering. Page 97.
2. Ride Height – reduce. Page 68.
3. Side Springs – softer. Page 82.
4. Caster – reduce angle (if this adjustment is available to you). Page 47.
5. Reduce traction additive on front tyres. Page 92.
6. Glue front tyre sidewalls. Even a thin layer of glue helps stop the traction roll. This stiffens the sidewall and in some cases allows the tyre to slide on the glue rather than fold under the car. Gluing the front sidewalls will reduce steering and may be best used on high grip carpet.
7. Harder front tyres.
8. Roll Centre (front) – raise. Page 77.

Troubleshooting

Car 'Hops' or 'Chatters' Across the Track

If the car 'hops' (also called 'chatter' or 'judder') when cornering, then the Springs are too stiff (refer to Springs on page 79).

Car Wanders on the Straight

Toe Out – increase.

Tyres Picking Up Carpet Debris from Track

This is normally only an issue on the front tyres where the part of the tyre with traction additive is fine, but the unsauced tyre is picking up significant carpet debris, reducing steering partway through the race. To resolve, add traction additive to the rest of the front tyre and then reduce steering either by:
1. Refer to Too Much Steering checklist on page 148, or
2. Add CA glue to the sidewall of the front tyres which will take away steering.

Inconsistent Handling

The following issues can also cause inconsistent handling:

1. If the rear pod does not move completely freely in all directions (refer to page *100*).
2. Foam Tyres – Left and right tyres are not close to the same diameter. If the tyre diameter on the left front is significantly different (more than 0.4mm) to the right front, or if the left rear is significantly different to the right rear, then this may be a contributing factor to an ill-handling car.
3. Battery wires, ESC motor wires, motor sensor wire, should not bind with the body on or off the car when the rear pod moves in any direction (refer to page *100*).
4. Kingpins should move up and down smoothly when the front suspension is compressed. If not, then check the kingpins are smooth (polish if needed), are not bent (replace) and have the correct lubrication (refer to Front Springs & Lube on page *81*).
5. If front kingpins do not have equal shimming on both sides or if too many shims are installed causing the spring to be over tensioned (refer to page *81*).
6. No play in balls for side links, but should move smoothly without binding (refer page *79*).
7. Track width shims are the same on the left as on the right (refer to page *89*).
8. Remove the front springs and place them next to each other on a flat surface. They should be the same length. Replace if needed. Repeat test for the side springs.

Lacking Acceleration or Started Oversteering

If the car was working well but is now lacking acceleration or has started oversteering then:

1. Ball differential may be slipping too much. Tighten using the recommendations on page *55*.
2. Check the screw that holds the diff/spur onto the rear axle. It may have come loose, or if using a carbon axle it may have become worn, allowing the spur to spin without driving the axle.

Quick Reference

After Run Checks	143
Change of Direction (Chicane)	144
Easier to Drive – How To	144
Fast Sweeper Cornering	145
New Car – How to Set Up	145
Re-building a Car	146
Rear Traction – How to Increase	147
Steering	148
Too Much Steering (Oversteer)	148
General Oversteer	148
Oversteer at Corner Entry	148
Oversteer at Mid-corner	148
Oversteer at Corner Exit	149
Oversteer On-power	149
Not Enough Steering (Understeer)	149
General Understeer	149
Understeer at Corner Entry	149
Understeer at Mid-corner	150
Understeer at Corner Exit or at High Speed	150
Steering Response Changes for No Apparent Reason	150
Traction Rolling	151
Troubleshooting	151
Car 'Hops' or 'Chatters' Across the Track	151
Car Wanders on the Straight	151
Tyres Picking Up Carpet Debris from Track	151
Inconsistent Handling	152
Lacking Acceleration or Started Oversteering	152

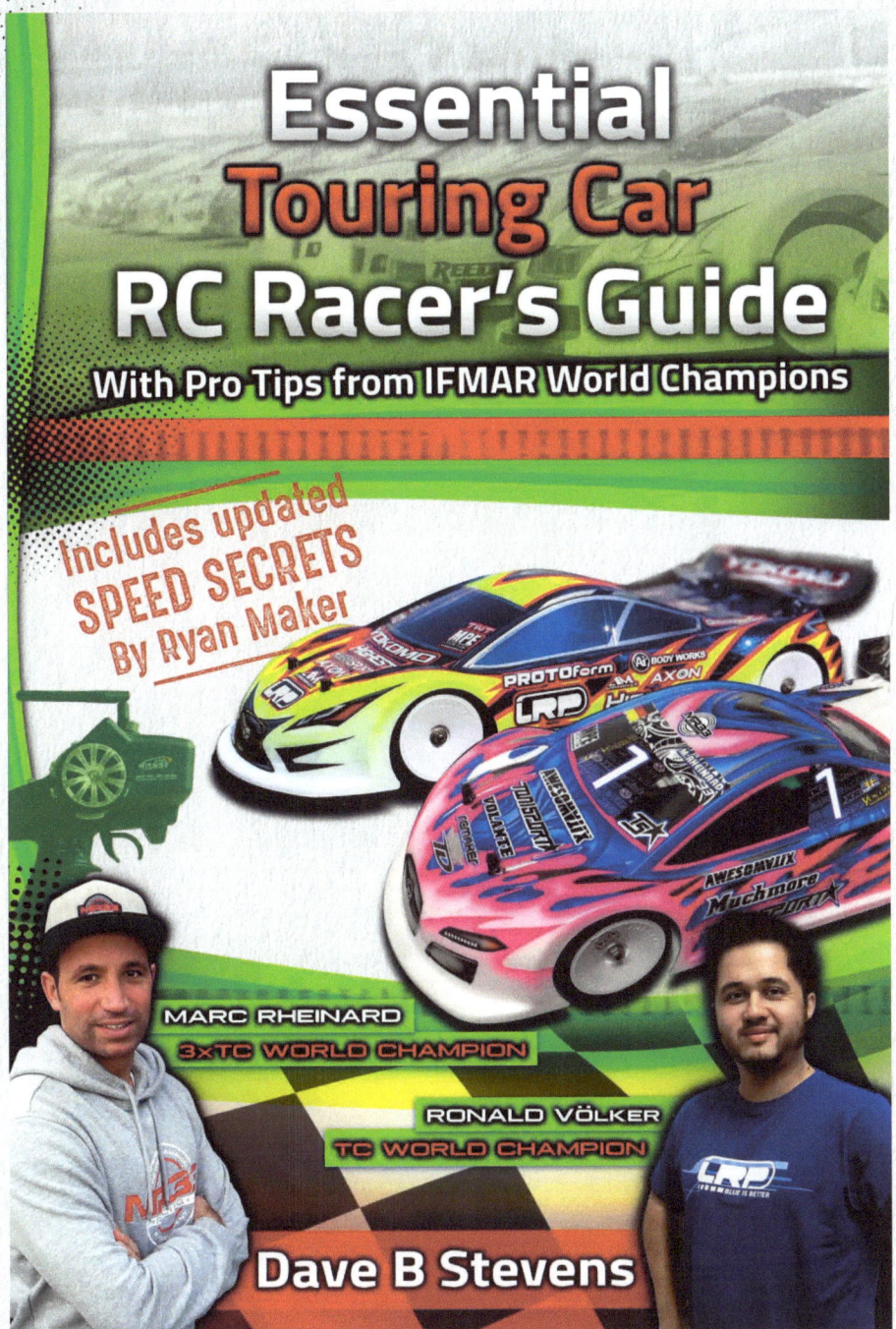

www.ingramcontent.com/pod-product-compliance
Lightning Source LLC
Chambersburg PA
CBHW041459010526
44107CB00044B/1504